Freaky Tuesday & other stories

A collection of short stories by

Dewi Heald

First published by Dream Jellyhouse in print on demand in 2018

Copyright ©Dewi Heald 2018

Photography Copyright © Dewi Heald 2018

The right of Dewi Heald to be identified as the Author of the Work has been asserted by him in accordance with the Copyright, Designs and Patents Act 1988.

All rights reserved

ISBN : 978-1-9995807-1-1

Dream Jellyhouse logo by DesignMantic

Dedication

This book is dedicated to Non Humphries,

who has read it all before

Index

This is Not About Ellie...........6
Athena by Lisa...........29
Selfies...........44
I'd Do Anything...........55
Freaky Tuesday...........67
The Dating Questionnaire...........92
Big Decisions...........96
The Wrong Sister...........118
God's Filing Card System...........124
Vegan Cheese...........144
The Tale of Charlotte the Liberator...........156
From Wow to Ow...........169
The Orange Hoodie...........173
   Darryl Fowler and the Mistaken Identity Case...........201
AFTERWORD...........221

please do not colour in this page

This is Not About Ellie

"Simon! You have five minutes! Shift!"

Madison Staples hugged her husband in the hallway of their house when she heard this.

"Thanks – you're okay to take them to school?" she asked.

"'Course – they just need to shift," he replied, kissing her gently on the forehead.

Maddie stood back and seemed to grow in size as she took in the air to shout up the stairs herself.

"Simon! Matthew! Your father's not joking, he'll take you to school naked if he has to!"

They hugged again.

"You going to be all right?" he asked her and then, standing back as if he was seeing her for the first time that morning, "You're looking every inch the professional biographer."

Maddie punched him playfully on the arm and replied, "You have no idea how a biographer dresses! Neither do I, mind you but ... yeah, bit nervous about first meeting with Mr Abraham today."

"Just remember, everyone's faking it in every job they do. You'll be great."

"I've done my research," said Maddie, tapping her laptop bag rather needlessly, "and anyway, I've also got to stop off at college and then the office, so it's just another detail of my day."

There was a crash from one of the upstairs bedrooms and both parents looked up the stairs and then at each other with a sense of familiar foreboding.

"Go now while you can!" said Maddie's husband, "I've read your research notes, you know your stuff. You can tell me about it this evening. Ask him about Ellie."

"Yeah," said Maddie, opening the door with a little trepidation about not investigating the crashing sound, "I really want to know more about Ellie."

* * * * *

"Madeline! Come in!"

"It's a pleasure to meet you, Mr Abraham, but please do call me Maddie."

Mr Abraham stepped aside and let Madison into his house. She walked into the front room and he indicated a chair for her to sit in.

"Would you like a mug of tea to get things going?" he asked.

"Yes, yes thank you," she said with slight nervousness in her voice.

Maddie's eye was caught by the row of pictures and awards sitting on top of the mantelpiece. They were all slightly dusty she noticed, but then who polishes their awards? The pictures showed the story of Ben Abraham's life – shows, concerts, children, friends – and she went to pick one up. These were the things that people knew about him, she thought to herself, the public face they saw or the Wikipedia page that they read. She wanted to take a different angle. She did not realise that he was standing in the kitchen doorway watching her.

"My biographer can't resist research, even when she is waiting for tea?" he joked.

Maddie swung round to apologise but saw a twinkle in his eye that told her that he was only teasing her. He waved his arm as if giving her permission to look at his photos and she laughed to herself. Sure, the man with the mop of dark curly hair in those pictures was now balding and older but she could already feel that certain something that made people want to know him or at least watch him on stage. There was also a hint of mischieviousness in his voice which she could imagine had got him in to a lot of trouble when it was mixed with a dash of fame.

"Do you have any soya milk?" she asked, "Or almond milk would do."

Her subject looked slightly flustered for the first time.

"No, I only have cow's milk, I'm sorry – I'll make sure that I have some soya milk for your next visit."

Maddie smiled as she turned back to the mantelpiece. Her next visit indeed, she thought of this more as an exploratory meeting to see if she could write his biography. Would he know that she had never done this before? Would the publishers have told him that she had answered an advert and was only doing this around college and her job? At least, that was how she started. Always a thorough woman, she had done her research and was now genuinely interested in the man. She returned to looking at the photos of the great Ben Abraham at his most famous.

Ben fussed with the kettle and the tea things. His initial assessment was good. The publishers had only agreed to this project when he promised to finance it himself and so he was pleased to see that his money was well-spent. So far Maddie Staples seemed to have that mixture of intelligence and attractiveness that could be so devastating. He would never tell her this of course, no-one wants a man in his sixties commenting on the looks of someone thirty years younger but all the same ... that combination could be dangerous for any man, it reminded him of Ellie.

"This is not about Ellie!" he said firmly and out loud, banging the kettle back on to its stand a little too firmly.

Maddie appeared at the door to the kitchen.

"Are you okay Mr Abraham?" she asked.

"Please, please, Ben," he replied, "and yes, yes, fine. Here – your tea. Sorry about the milk, animals were harmed in its production."

"Thank you," she said and they walked back into the front room and relaxed on separate sofas.

Ben had worried that the publishers would not take the biography project seriously. His suspicions seemed to have been confirmed when he learnt that Maddie was juggling another job and going to college to retrain for a qualification in Travel and Tourism. However, they convinced him that she had a reasonable background of writing online and that she had research skills. He also suspected that she was the cheap option and that they were taking a sizable cut from his donation to the project. In meeting her she seemed intelligent, attractive and determined. She was definitely the right person for the job of his life. He just had to set down some rules for her.

"How do you want to do this?" he asked, pretending that he did not know that this was her first time.

Maddie took out a small laptop from her backpack, opened it up on the coffee table and also brought out a hand-sized mini notebook with scribbled writing on the top page.

"I wondered if you could give me some key experiences or ideas to hang the story on," she said, "it's a nice place you have here, by the way."

"Oh yes," Ben said awkwardly, "too big for me on my own really, but hard to find anywhere where I can store the musical instruments. My Dad was like that too. Weird how when you reach old age you realise how little variation there is in our DNA."

Maddie typed a few sentences and then looked up with caution on her face.

"This is an authorized biography, of course, so you can have some direction in how it is written. I'd prefer as much freedom as you can give me but, otherwise, is there any special instruction?"

Ben Abraham looked away from her to his row of awards, brought out of the spare room and arranged in more prominent view only that morning.

"I don't want you to mention Ellie," he said.

Maddie looked up from her notes and shook her head with a puzzled look.

"She seems to have been a big part of your life, you can't really write her out."

"No, you can write her out," he said, an odd cloud floating across his sunny disposition, "from the moment I meet her in Swansea through to the final goodbye in Llandovery, I want no mention of her. She is not important to the story - to my story."

They stared at each other for a moment and then his face relaxed, the cloud passed and the sun shone again.

"I saw that photo on your mantelpiece," she said, pointing across to a picture half-hidden behind a postcard of Sao Miguel.

Ben stood up slightly stiffly and walked over to it. Maddie smiled as she watched him do it because it occurred to her that his well-cut jacket and suit trousers had been specially chosen for the interview. Of course, someone who was a performer would always be a performer, even for his biographer. He was holding the picture in his hands now. It showed him standing on stage in Las Vegas, in front of a band, conducting his audience in a singalong. His face is half-obscured by his arm but you could see the intensity of the expression. Maddie had seen it before in her research and it was her favourite picture of him. He looked so totally alive.

"What were you feeling at that moment?" she asked.

Ben turned around and looked at her in surprise at the question. He was expecting her to ask about the song or the concert or even the band, but not his feelings. He placed the photo back on the mantelpiece and smoothed his hands down over his jacket.

"That was just the best," he admitted, "the best moment of my life, I suppose. I know, I should probably say the birth of my children, but to be honest ... this was when everything just came together, it was the peak. Oh okay, the best moment so far, if you insist. But I'm in my sixties now, this next act won't be anything like the last ones."

Ben walked back to the sofa and sat next to his mug of tea, He sipped it and thought some more. Maddie was waiting for him to say more and left the silence there for him to jump into.

"I had done other people's songs, of course. People hear you sing a Sinatra song and they're always thinking of Sinatra somewhere in their mind. My own songs though ... I had written that one ... well, just the sound of people singing your own words back to you. 'Hazy Autumn' it was, written as I was driving through Ceredigion one day. At the end of a relationship and ... well, it never worked when I first played it and then someone suggested making it an audience singalong."

Maddie simply smiled and typed as he spoke. He was not looking at her, he was looking somewhere off into the distance beyond the curtains.

"Oh yes," she said deliberately and provocatively, "that song was written about the end of your relationship with ..."

Ben's gaze fixed back on her. She did not need to complete the sentence.

"She didn't write it though. Do you praise the man who sells you a hot dog before you climb the Eiffel Tower?"

"I've never been to Paris," she said, flatly.

"Yes well, I haven't either. Well, I spent a day there on the way to a gig in Brussels. They liked my kind of jazz in Belgium."

"Tell me more about Belgium then," said Maddie, typing carefully.

* * * * *

"Eleanor Tamarind, known as Ellie," pondered Maddie as the food cooked slowly on the oven in front of her, "how are the boys?"

"They're okay," said her husband distractedly, focussing on typing on the laptop on the kitchen table.

"He meets her in Swansea when he barely has a career, they are together around ten years during which he rises to fame and makes it big. They split up. He then meets Cath and has his children. Yet he never seems to forget Ellie. Cath is interesting in her own way, but there was never anything about Ellie which wasn't exciting and interesting."

Maddie's husband looked up from his work.

"That's why he hasn't forgotten her. He's on his own now so he's going back to the best times for memories."

"Do you think our best times are behind us? I mean, shouldn't you always believe that there is better to come?" she asked.

Maddie's husband shut down his laptop and shook his head.

"The kids are too quiet, I'll go and check," he said.

"Thanks, I've got an essay for college to finish tonight, don't forget."

* * * * *

"Madeline!" said Ben, as he opened the door.

"Mr Abraham."

They had become accustomed to this greeting and neither corrected the other. Ben had already started the kettle boiling for her tea. Maddie hung her heavy winter coat up by the front door, removed her boots and placed them on the shoe rack inside the front room and walked in. On her first couple of visits she had found paddling around in her thick winter socks rather odd, but she was used to it now.

Maddie placed her backpack down on the coffee table and took out her laptop. It could warm up as she warmed up – Mr Abraham was not a man who had to skimp on heating his house.

Maddie wandered over to the bookcase in the corner of the room. She had noticed it before, but not had the chance to really look at the books. Books seemed even more special to her these days. If someone read, then they might well read on e-readers and tablets so the books that they chose to keep on paper, they must be important to them.

She ran her finger along the spine of mystery stories, a couple of thrillers and some histories and biographies.

Music was a theme, of course, biographies of musicians, books on music theory and even a couple of thrillers where the hero is a musician. There was a cheap, plastic kazoo on the shelf too and she could not resist blowing on it.

"You haven't passed the audition, I'm afraid," said Ben, appearing in the kitchen doorway with two big mugs of tea, "you need to hum rather than blow."

"Sorry, I was just ..." she started with a smile.

"Oh, no bother. You thinking that for someone who didn't show much interest in the library in school, I have a lot of books?"

"No, I ... hold on, what's this?"

Maddie's glance was caught by a spine that she recognised but did not expect to see. She pulled out a copy of a 'romance novel for women' that had caused a big sensation ten years before but which was now mostly seen on the sale rack in charity book shops. They were never particularly good, but they always sold well because there was so little mainstream pornography aimed at women and something that promised explicit scenes told from a woman's point of view would do well. This one had had the gimmick that the main character would see the potential sex life she could have with a man just by shaking his hand. It was nonsense of course, but it made for a lot of different sexual scenarios written up in rather predictable – and very successful – scenes. 'Now a major motion picture' screamed a red sticker on the front of the book and she remembered how dire that was as well.

"Did you prefer the book or the film?" he asked with a smile.

"Oh, I only vaguely remember this," she replied, "but I'm really intrigued to find it on your bookshelf. It should at least be in the charity shop with every other copy sold that summer."

Ben laughed and shook his head.

"It was a present. Well, it was more something someone leant me and then never wanted back. I hated reading at school – you know of course, we covered this all last time – but I wanted to catch up on all that when I had time on my hands to do it. Yeah, at 16 I would have said 'I don't read no books me and proud of it' but at 66 ..."

"You read women's soft core porn?"

Ben laughed and Maddie picked up her laptop to work out where to start asking questions. She was finding that rather than go through his life in order, it worked better if she asked him for significant moments and drew themes and ideas from that. She had worked out already that he had hated school, had left at sixteen to become an apprentice bricklayer and that he did early gigs billed as 'the singing brickie'. That transformation from labourer to musician leading the audience in a singalong in Las Vegas was fascinating to her but she still found it hard to connect the two lives.

"Tell me more about Amelia Wallace," she said.

"Mel? Well ... what can I say? When I first met her she had dyed her hair blue at the back. It was black hair with blue flames coming out of it I thought at the time. She had one of those bright, attentive faces and dark eyes that ..."

"Ben?" she said, to stop him, "I have photos of her."

"Oh, sorry Maddie, sorry. It's too much fun picturing these things in my mind. You want details. Mel then ... well, I'd been singing for a while, had that initial success as the Singing Brickie. We were at the jazz night in Sutherland's on St Mary's Street, a mutual friend sang in a bossanova band and ..."

"Why was she 'Amelia' but shortened it to 'Mel' rather than 'Meel'?"

"I don't know."

"Funny that."

"She said 'why don't you ask the band if you could do a number?'" he continued, undeterred, "I was never bold enough for it but, when I hesitated, she went and introduced herself to the lead singer and said that I was a great singer and I wanted to do some Brazilian jazz."

"You were never bold enough? That's surprising," said Maddie as she typed.

"I am more shy that you would expect," he said, with a nervous smile, "but yes, she got me to sing there and through that I met Rebecca Filmore who got the first recording deal and was an ace with publicity ..."

"And all because you met Meel."

"Yes, she really changed my life."

"And who introduced the two of you?" said Maddie, not looking up.

Ben stood up and walked over to the mantelpiece to look at his photos again. He might be an old man sitting in a ground floor flat somewhere in a jumper, waiting for his children to phone if it had not been for all this. It had taken so much work too. Work that he had put into it, work that he had believed in and no-one else.

"Yes, it was Ellie who introduced us. We went for a night out in Swansea at some point and she got talking to Mel and they hit it off. But it was after she left – she cheated on me, you know – long after she left that Mel helped me, so no, it's not thanks to Ellie."

"Yet, if it wasn't for her, then you wouldn't have met Meel and ..."

"She cheated on me, you do know that? She cheated on me more than once."

"I've heard the songs about it."

"Songs I wrote! I rang her, you know? I rang her from Ceredigion and do you know what I said?"

"You said 'wow, I'm in Ceredigion and I have phone reception!'?"

"Well, obviously but, you know, after that. I told her that I had written a song about her cheating on me and our relationship ending as autumn and brown leaves and ... well, she didn't even appreciate it."

"It was hardly a love song."

Ben turned back from the mantelpiece and returned to the sofa. He sighed as an indication that he was not going to talk about it. Maddie was clever, she would work out that the timing did not work in his story and that he must have met Mel while he was still with Ellie.

Let her work it out, he could always edit it out in the final proof copy. He had to remember that he was in control of how she wrote about his life. He smiled again.

"I'm sorry Maddie," he said, "I shouldn't have got annoyed. Let me tell you about how those gigs in the Sutherland led to recording. Oh and the John Lewis ad – that really was a lucky break ..."

On her laptop, Maddie wrote how odd it was that a man who clearly had looks and who had a great deal of charm could have ended up single. It seemed to her to be one of the conundrums of his career. He had children and he had had partners but he was also hardly the groupie-loving playboy either. He was someone who wanted to settle down, the averageness of the house spoke of a home away from his fame and she felt as though he had always been like that. She wrote that even the most eligible of people can end up alone. Then she crossed it out. It was important for her to believe that people such as herself who were married were the eligible ones and that those who ended up alone had some flaw.

* * * * *

"Last visit!" said Maddie cheerily as she stepped in the front door and then turned to shake off her umbrella.

"Everyone should have a biographer," replied Ben, taking her coat from her back and hanging it on a hook, "give them a chance to talk about themselves."

Maddie slipped off her ankle boots and Ben put them on the shoe rack for her. It had not been long into their meetings that she had decided that he was lonely and that she was partly his way of having someone to talk to about his life. She wondered about those children in the photos on the mantelpiece and why they did not phone him more often.

"Oh, you've never come across as egotistical at all," she said, "You always sound genuinely amazed at your life. Touch of impostor syndrome I have to say – how can a lad like me from a run down terrace become famous and ... well, not rich, but you always held on to your money, it was never fast cars and women with expensive tastes, was it?"

Ben pointed needlessly for her to walk into the front room and then watched her move in front of him. For their final meeting she had chosen dark tights and a black dress with the occasional bright flower across it. It was almost like mourning with a touch of jollity thrown in. He had been dressing to look smart for these interviews ... chats ... talks ... what were they exactly? He was going to miss her.

"I always thought that it could all go tomorrow. Still do really. Anything - fate like a hurricane coming in and blowing everything away. I still stash every royalty cheque – well, it's all electronic now but you know what I mean. I was always generous with friends but never with myself. Then again, I only ever achieved anything because of the wonderful people around me."

Maddie laughed and sat down in her usual seat.

"Philosophy before tea? That's not the Abraham way!"

"You're right!" he said and disappeared to make her the usual large tea, with soya milk bought in specially for her.

"Are you nearly done?" a voice called out from the kitchen.

For a minute Maddie wondered what on earth he was talking about. Then she realised that he meant done with the biography. She would miss him too, for all that there was a career, a part-time course, a husband and two children waiting for her in the rest of the world. She knew so much about him now that when she looked at the photo of Las Vegas, it almost seemed to move and, more than that, she was in the audience singing along, marvelling at the skill with which he held them in the palm of his hand. What must it be like to be the man who had once done that?

"Can I have a look around?" she asked, "You know, final visit, get one last feel of how you live."

"Sure," came the reply from the kitchen and Maddie made her way to the upstairs of the house.

It was a modest upper floor – there was a small bathroom at the end, its shelf filled with male grooming products that said that he still took his appearance seriously. Then there was a music room, it must have been a bedroom originally, but filled with all sorts of instruments. She imagined that he still went in there from time to time and picked out a tune that reminded him of former days. Then there was his bedroom. Maddie felt rude looking in there, but it was part of who he was, where he relaxed. She was not sure why and she was trying to avoid sexist stereotypes as she thought this, but she imagined that it was 'a man's house'. She was not sure what touch a woman would bring to it, but there was something missing. In fact, that was just like her biography of him. It had all the facts about his music, his determination and his pride, but there was something missing.

Maddie paused for a moment on the stairs. There were two pictures hanging on the wall, both advertised shows that he had done twenty years before. How odd to be surrounded by reminders that you were once popular and interesting, she thought. Were they reminders of how much he had achieved or did they admonish him for being lesser than that now? Was his comment in the first meeting right – did he know that he had lived the best moment of his life and, if so, why would he continue on now?

She shuddered and walked back downstairs. She knew that she had to address the missing section of his biography. Ben was waiting for her, sitting on the sofa as ever, smartly dressed as ever and having made mugs of tea for them as ever.

"There's something I need to tell you," she said, sitting down and taking a slurp of tea, "and you're not going to like it."

"Oh dear," he said with a slight smile, "have you concluded I'm some kind of arse?"

"Not at all," Maddie said with a laugh, "not at all. I have to say that it is only because I am being funded by the anonymous donor that I feel that I have the freedom to say this."

"Ah yes, the anonymous donor," replied Ben, "did you never wonder who he was?"

"I always assumed one of your biggest fans."

"I wouldn't call him that," sighed Ben, but waved for her to continue.

"You keep telling me not to mention Ellie. Every now and then we go down a path here or there but we end up at a locked gate because she was the one who gave you the lead. Hell, that poster up there from the Birmingham NEC gig – you only ever had the contact there because Ellie knew someone. I've read up about it."

"But it's not about her. We dated. We were happy together yes, but then she went off with that idiot who couldn't even hold a tune. I don't want her to be part of my story. She's not here, isn't that enough to explain it?" he said testily.

"She's not here, but she's the Ellie in the room that no-one talks about! You have a picture of your glory days on the stairs, but you might as well have a picture of her and tell me that your best days are past."

Ben did not know whether to laugh or remain angry so he simply shook his head, sat back in the sofa and said no more.

"I thought of that 'Ellie in the room' thing upstairs," she added, "I thought that it was quite good. Perhaps I should be a lyricist?"

"Go on then, if you're not frightened of offending your mystery backer, tell me about Ellie."

Maddie had not really expected him to invite her to continue, but she had prepared what she wanted to say.

"Ellie was part of your life. You spent a long time – years – with her and yes, it ended badly, but you are not a stupid man, you would not have stayed with her if it was always bad. People always say at the end of relationships, 'oh that was five years of my life wasted' or whatever but I know now what rubbish it is. There are so many bits of your life where Ellie has been an influence, helped you out, got you talking to the right person ... I don't know."

"And I should be thankful to her?"

"No, you owe her nothing, but be honest. Even the bad things inspired you. That's life. It's good, it's bad, but you made good things out of the bad things as well as the good things. If you include her in your life, you are not taking away from what you have achieved. You know what, now I think about it, there's no relationship that's all bad."

Ben raised his eyebrows at her to ask if that was really true and she shrugged as if to say she knew that there were obvious exceptions for violence, abuse and other extreme cases though, when she thought about it, even those could build resilience in people.

She continued : "You can't tell your life story without the bad as well as the good. You can't just write her out. That relationship is part of you. If you regret it, you regret part of yourself."

Ben looked as though he was thinking about this. He leaned forwards as he did so and picked an orange out of the fruit bowl on the coffee table. He peeled it idly as if he simply needed something to keep his hands busy while he thought.

"They're like scars?" he asked, not looking at her.

"Tattoos I was thinking."

"We can't agree on a metaphor."

"Just let me write your biography with her in it and then, if you don't like it, you can always take it out. You can always fight it out with your mystery backer."

"Okay," he said, "but it's not about Ellie, it's about me."

Maddie said nothing but typed on her laptop.

* * * * *

Madison Staples walked into her bedroom and shut the door behind her. Her husband looked up from the tablet he was holding in his lap.

"Finished?" he asked.

"I told you not to read that thing in bed," she said evenly as she walked round to her side of the bed and climbed in, "but yes, it's done, I think. I'll do a final proof-read but otherwise, that's my first biography."

Danny Staples leaned over and kissed his wife on the forehead and then went back to looking at his tablet.

"Does that mean we can take his CDs off the player?" he asked, not looking up.

"No! I've enjoyed those! I only bought them as background but, yes, I like them."

Danny looked over at her and put his tablet down on his bedside table.

"I just don't think I'm a Belgian jazz guy or whatever it is. That 'Hazy Autumn' album you played me mind, I could swear that woman was dead the way he writes about her. He can write mind, I'll give you that. There's something he sings about seeing her favourite pizza in the supermarket and it should be really naff but that kind of worked for me."

Maddie snuggled up next to him and thought about this for a few moments.

"I did think about trying to find her, Ellie I mean. It's odd, isn't it? He still misses her. You imagine that somewhere he has a note she wrote saying 'Gone shopping, back later to give you a big snog'."

"He was married after he knew her, you know."

Maddie sat up and hit her husband lightly on the arm.

"I'm his biographer, remember!"

"Yeah, yeah, yeah," said Danny, "I mean, remember when we first got together and you wouldn't let me even mention Debra."

"Ah yes, Zebra," said Maddie, emphasising the incorrect pronunciation to indicate her lack of respect for the woman, "but that was different, I thought she fancied you."

"She didn't fancy me, she wanted to kill me," replied Danny, switching out the light on his bedside table, leaving only his wife's shining across the bedroom.

"Exactly, she fancied you. Believe me, women only have the time to plan to kill men they find attractive."

"Well then," said Danny, turning to look at her thoughtfully, "what if he was never allowed to talk about Ellie so he kept this interest in her and now it comes out as this disowning of any influence on him? You know, why can't we all accept that other people were part of people's lives? I never questioned all the Garys you dated before you met me!"

Maddie lay in silence for a moment contemplating this. There were not that many Garys, certainly not enough to be referred to collectively, she felt.

"What was Zebra's favourite kind of pizza?" she asked.

"Hawaiian - ham and pineapple."

"Ha!" snorted Maddie contemptuously, "she put pineapple on pizza, I knew that I had nothing to fear from her!"

"Come on, switch the light out, it's late," said Danny and Maddie rolled over and pressed the switch on the small light on her bedside table. Now the only light was a thin sliver of orange thrown across the bed by a street light outside.

"I just can't imagine thinking that the best of your life has already gone," murmured Maddie in the dark, "not just in your career but in relationships too. The best you has passed."

Danny did not answer but took her into his arms and they lay together for a while not saying anything but feeling the comfort and re-assurance of each other's warmth. Then Maddie rolled over to face the window so that Danny could cuddle her from behind.

There was a sudden loud crush of drums and trumpets and a voice singing about leaves turning brown. Maddie's arms started scrambling around under the bed clothes.

"Damn! Damn! Damn! I rolled onto the remote."

She quickly found it and switched the music off.

"I'm changing the CD tomorrow," said Danny, "we're going back to rock ballads. Another few moments of that and he would be talking about pizza."

"Mmm ..." said Maddie as she settled down into his cuddle again, "can we have pizza tomorrow night?"

"Yeah, sure," replied Danny, "you should try it with pineapple on."

"Shut up."

Athena by Lisa

Greg sat down heavily next to Sylvia on the same commuter train service that he had caught for the last twenty years. Twenty years younger than him, Sylvia had barely started school when he first caught that train but she looked up from the free newspaper and nodded acknowledgement of his arrival. They worked in the same office and that was connection enough for him to sit next to her. She shuffled over to one side as he spread out on the seat next to her.

"What you doing?" he asked, peering over her shoulder.

"Reading the cartoons - I like 'Athena by Lisa'," she replied.

"I never get that stuff," he said, as if his opinion was important to her.

Sylvia folded the 'paper over and pointed to the cartoon strip.

"This is Athena and it's all about her life. Sometimes it's about her work, sometimes it's about her family ... she has these two men after her, one is kind of casual and the other is all romantic and ..."

"She's sexy, that's for sure," said Greg, interrupting her without thinking about it.

"She's strong and sexy, that's the thing," said Sylvia, regarding him with a slightly contemptuous frown, "She's not 'sexy but weak and indecisive'. Anyway, you can't fancy a cartoon character."

"You can when she's drawn like that! She's always wearing those big boots or those short skirts or tight tops! I mean, not that I do. I mean ... look, I don't get it. Why doesn't she make up her mind about those two men?"

Sylvia put the folded newspaper on her lap and sighed.

"Neither of them make her their priority. She would probably go for whichever of them did that, but neither treats her as important so she never feels like she has to choose."

"I still don't get it. Doesn't she have superpowers or something?"

Sylvia laughed to herself. For a man who knew nothing about the cartoon in the newspaper, Greg seemed to know quite a lot about Athena and her life. She wondered if he hid a copy of it up his jumper every morning and snuck away to a secret part of the office to read it.

They were quiet as some more commuters squeezed around them at the next stop. The train had certainly become busier in the last twenty years, in fact even in the last year when Sylvia had been catching it.

"It's not like she's a superhero or anything, she gets a power each week. Look, this is today's ..."

Sylvia unfolded the newspaper again and pointed to the strip.

"She starts by saying she wishes that she knew what other people were thinking. Then she gets the power to hear people's thoughts and guess what, she finds out how much they are judging her and she decides that she is better off not knowing," explained Sylvia, pointing at each panel.

"What's funny about that?" asked Greg, peering carefully and then looking away in disgust.

"If you were a woman, you would understand," replied Sylvia with a sigh.

"In my day, it was situation, development and then laugh. Where's the laugh in that?"

Greg shook his head as if young people did not understand comedy, along with all the other things that they did not understand. Sylvia was pretty and young, but sometimes she was odd, he thought. More commuters entered the carriage and now the people standing were being pushed into the seated people. They really did need to have more carriages on these trains in the mornings.

After a minute or two of silence, Greg spoke without looking at Sylvia.

"I just think that the bloke who draws that Athena must really fancy her or something."

"'By Lisa'?" she asked, not looking back.

"Probably a bloke in disguise," he muttered.

* * * * *

Lisa Gutteridge looked up from her drawing table in her studio flat when she heard the sound in the entrance hallway. Dammit, Jake was early and she still did not have the final drawing done on the latest Athena strip. She looked at the clock. Six o'clock already? She had spent too long drawing the panel where Athena is leaving the ground. She wanted to feel her freedom though and she lingered on the distance between Athena's boots and the earth.

Jake had soon taken the spare key out of the plant pot and was letting himself into the front room. She called out a greeting to him without looking up from her drawing. She heard the sound of his shoes crossing the wooden floor and then felt his arms wrap around her from behind and then his cool breath on her neck.

"How's my favourite little artist?" he asked.

"Get off," she said gently as he kissed her neck, "I'm still not finished".

"Are you sure I can't persuade you to take a break?" he said, running his hands under her loose-fitting top and cupping her breasts.

"Off!" she said more firmly this time, shaking her shoulders so that he withdrew his hands and stepped away from her.

"Okay, okay!" he said with a laugh, "I know where I'm not wanted."

Lisa swung round on her high chair and brushed some of her long, brown hair away from her face. She silently castigated her nipples for having hardened under his touch. Dammit, she really should have made more of an effort before he arrived. She worked in these loose-fitting linen clothes and with bare feet, but perhaps she should try to be more attractive for him.

"I haven't finished this week's strip," she said, holding her ink pen up as if he needed to see it to understand what she was saying, "make yourself at home - the food is in the kitchen if you want to get it cooking."

"Nah, you're all right," he said and sat down on the sofa behind her, "I'll watch some telly while you finish up."

She looked at him for a moment. What could she say about Jake? Attractive and sexy, but also damn lazy.

"What you working on anyway?" he said, without looking at her, fixating instead on which remote control would take him to a more interesting TV channel, "What's the superpower thing?"

"Athena is flying this week, it's kind of lovely."

"Why?" he said, still not looking up.

Lisa swung back around on her chair and ran a hand across the cartoon strip laid out in front of her. She was almost stroking it.

"All these people. They're telling her what to do and what she should be and so on. They keep telling her that she has to make a choice so she just flies away. Just lifts off and flies away from them all."

Jake shrugged his shoulders and said, "So she avoids making a decision? Thought you said she was some hero to 'women in the twenty to thirty demographic'?"

He said those last words with the sound of sarcasm, as if he had never really accepted that she drew something that was read by tens of thousands of people every morning.

"Athena's not evading responsibility, she's escaping people who want to tell her what to do. She knows that the only person whose decision matters is hers and she doesn't want them all telling her what to think, what to do, what to feel ..."

Lisa's voice trailed off as she looked at the strip, resting her hand by it protectively. There were just a few more lines to fill in and then she would sign it as her property. Jake was already looking at the television and not paying attention to her.

"Are you listening to me?" she asked.

"Yeah, I am, I am," he lied, realising that he had to cover up his error by changing the subject, "Anyway, I know that I'm Tim."

"What do you mean?" asked Lisa, walking over to the sofa to sit next to him.

"I'm Tim - the guy in your cartoons who Athena fancies but who never commits to her. I know that. He's the casual one," said Jake, putting an arm around her.

Lisa felt the warmth of his body next to hers and sighed with satisfaction.

"You're not. None of them are based on anyone. Creative people take bits of people they know and put them together into new people."

"Like Frankenstein?" he asked, with a laugh in his voice.

Lisa punched his stomach gently.

"Not like Frankenstein, like someone being creative and creating a better world," she said.

They had food and snuggled up on the sofa together again afterwards. After a while watching an old sci-fi series, they went upstairs to Lisa's modest bedroom and had sex. It was not earth-shattering, mind-blowing sex, but she felt glad for this attractive man in her bed and they lay together in the darkness afterwards, lost in their own thoughts.

Lisa reached out under the duvet and touched his hand. As she made contact, she felt all bar one part of his body stiffen, as if the intimacy was frightening. She held on and felt his body relax as he held her hand. After a while, he spoke out into the silence of the room.

"She's you, you know."

"Who is?" said Lisa, rolling over to look at him.

Jake turned to face her. Even in the darkness of the room, she thought that he looked slightly nervous and guilty to be saying it.

"Athena. She's you or rather, she's the you that you want to be."

"Rubbish. She's nothing like me. She's strong and sexy and powerful."

"That's why you dress her to look so attractive, it's because you'd like to dress in a way that attracts men too."

"She does not dress to attract people!" said Lisa, sitting up and letting go of his hand with anger in her voice, "She dresses like that because it makes her feel attractive. If other people are attracted to her then that's nothing to do with her. She dresses to please herself!"

Jake sat up and placed a hand on her shoulder. He felt that she was shaking slightly and he waited for her to calm down without saying any words. There was a faint sliver of light coming from the street lamps and it poked through the curtains and fell on to the side of her face.

"But if she dresses like that, she must know that it will attract men. Look anyway, that's not what I'm saying. I just think that you want to be her."

Lisa peered at him and even in that little light she could see that he was sincere.

"She's just a cartoon character," she said after a while.

"She's your cartoon character, why don't you give her the power to get into the real world or something. I don't know. If she's who you want to be, you could try being her or something. Look, I don't know, but ..."

Somewhere in that strange tumble of words, she knew that any minute now he would be gathering up his clothes and heading home. She had been just starting to enjoy the conversation as well. That was always the point when the sudden end of the evening surprised and hurt her in the darkness.

"I've got work in the morning ..." he started.

* * * * *

Jake could not find the spare key under the plant pot. It was the same pot, the same hallway, the same studio flat in there with its big expanse of open living space with bedroom space up a staircase at one side of the room. Everything was the same except for the key that he should be using to let himself in. He knocked on the door.

"Lisa!" he called, "I can't find the key!"

After a little wait where he started to wonder if there was anyone in the flat at all, the door opened and he saw a woman standing in the doorway. It was Lisa, but dressed in black boots, a short black skirt and a tight red top. She had slicked her hair back and tied it behind her head and she had taken some time on her make up. His first thought was 'wow'.

"Lisa!" he said, "You look gorgeous!"

She shrugged her shoulders and motioned him into the room, stepping to one side to avoid him trying to hug her.

"I'm still working," she said, "I have a bit more to do on this week's strip. It's going in a new direction, shall we say."

"Sure," he said, still surprised and turned on by the new look, "I'll just take a seat on the sofa and you tell me when ..."

"No," she said firmly, "you take a walk into the kitchen. I've got everything set up for tonight's meal and there's some instructions. I'll come and help in a minute when I'm done working."

Jake stared at her for a moment. He had no idea what to say. His routine with Lisa had been so set that both her new outfit and her new attitude amazed him.

It also annoyed him. Who was she to tell him what to do? He was used to ... she was staring at him from her high drawing chair.

"Sure Lisa," he said, not really knowing what else to say.

"Oh and Jake!" she called, without looking at him as she swung back to her drawing table, "the name's Athena."

Jake turned around to say something, but was not sure what to say. Was this some kind of new thing she was trying out? Was she trying to disprove his point about Athena being her other life? Her back was turned to him now and he felt too confused to know what to say, so he went into the kitchen as requested.

Jake spent some time in the kitchen nervously trying to follow the cooking instructions. To be fair to Lisa - Athena or whatever she wanted to call herself for this evening - she had prepared all the food and all he had to do was watch some pots, check the oven and make sure that it all came together. He smiled to himself as he realised that it was a lot easier than he had thought it would be.

He decided that she must have taken his comment about her wanting to be Athena to heart. It had been a week or two ago now and perhaps that moment, perhaps she decided to play some sort of game with him. He could do that. It would still be him popping over to her flat, spending some time with her, having sex and then not having to make any commitment. He could cope with that.

He realised that Athena had walked into the kitchen doorway and was looking at him. How she managed to do it quietly in those high boots he had no idea but he smiled at her and the shapely shadow thrown on to the wall behind her by the light. In her hand she still had one of her drawing pens.

"Doing stuff together, that's how it works," she said, "though I know why you're doing it."

"You got telepathy this week?" he joked.

Athena laughed and Jake smiled weakly back at her. She walked towards him steadily and looked at the meal that was being prepared.

"Have you done gravy?" she asked.

"Gravy?" he said with a hint of panic in his voice, "It's not in the instructions!"

"You can do it from the juices of the chicken. Ah, no worries, I'll do it. You can go relax for a moment."

He started to walk out of the kitchen but, as he did so, Athena reached out and pulled back on his shoulder to turn him around to face her.

Jake stood there surprised as she walked steadily towards him and then pushed him back against the wall. For a moment he wanted to object because it was almost time to take the roast potatoes out of the oven and then he wondered where the hell that thought had come from. He gasped as Athena unbuttoned the top buttons of his shirt. Then she stopped.

Taking a step backwards she brought her pen forwards and signed her name across the top of his chest. It was uneven across his hair and caught his collar bone on the top of the 'h' but it was a signature.

"What the hell?" he exclaimed.

"If you look in the mirror it will say 'anehtA'," she said with a smile.

"It's almost time for the roast potatoes to come out the oven," he stammered, really unsure of what else to say.

"You see," she continued, watching him as he opened the oven and removed the potatoes, "when you used to visit Lisa, you treated her as your property. I wondered how it would feel to you to be my property."

"This is weird!" he said, "I'm no-one's property!"

Athena laughed and pulled some plates out of a cupboard. She handed them to him and said softly, "And neither am I."

Over dinner, Athena talked about how the comic strip was developing and how people might not like its new direction. Jake nodded and told her about how things had been in the call centre where he worked. Occasionally he let his mind wander and watching her place a long parsnip between her red lips did cause him to become distracted more than once.

He seemed to have lost the art of what he thought of as being subtle. As he cleared away her plate, he placed a hand half way along her leg, on top of her skirt.

"Ah," she sighed, "a quick feel of the thigh, such a gentleman to offer to clear up!"

Jake looked awkward and embarrassed. Lisa never used to notice this kind of thing before.

"You need to understand," she continued, "that if we have sex tonight then it is because we both want it. You used to come around here expecting it from Lisa and you need to understand that those days have gone. That's why the key has gone from under the plant pot. In future, you need to phone."

* * * * *

Jake was lying on his back snoring heavily and Athena watched him sleep. Poor man, she thought, I have really tired him out. Maybe I will wake him in a while to see if he has recovered. Maybe I will let him sleep on.

Athena was not a stupid woman. She knew what all this meant and it meant nothing. A man who will check on the roast potatoes because he fancies you and thinks that he will get to have sex with you is not a man who loves you or a man who will ever put you first in his life. A man who really loves you would check on the roast potatoes whether you were wearing a short skirt or loose leggings. She rolled away from him to her bedside table and picked up her phone.

Looking over at Jake with a wry smile, she sent a text to Steve. Steve was the gentlemanly one. She would suggest a meal out somewhere, pleasant conversation, maybe a bottle of wine, an evening of sophistication.

What Athena really wanted though was a man who loved her and who she loved too. Someone who would put her first and who she would put first. Ah well, neither of them were that man, but she could have fun with them while she waited for him to come along. Would it be cruel if she told Jake about Steve? She laughed because for one moment she thought about waking him up now and telling him. That was too cruel though. She was no doormat like Lisa but she was also not cruel.

Jake mumbled something, woken by her laughter.

"Ah good," she said, "you're awake, let's not waste the time before I have to get to work."

Oh yes, they both knew that Lisa would never behave like this.

* * * * *

Greg sat down heavily on the seat next to Sylvia. Now the mornings were becoming lighter and he had a little bit more of a bounce to his step. For the last week or two, she always seemed to be sitting next to someone else by the time that the train arrived at his stop. Sylvia shuffled over to allow him to sit down.

"You reading those cartoons?" he asked, though it was obvious that she was reading those cartoons.

"Yeah, but they're not as good as they used to be," she replied, not looking up.

"I thought you liked that 'Athena by Lisa' thing? The superhero one with the woman who can fly?"

Sylvia folded up the newspaper and frowned at him.

"Funny thing happened a couple of weeks ago. It stopped being 'Athena by Lisa' and became 'Lisa by Athena'. The hero's this kind of wishy-washy woman who doesn't really make decisions and never dresses very well. I don't really like her much, to be honest."

"Thought you said that she was supposed to be a role model for twentysomethings or whatever?" asked Greg, genuinely puzzled.

Some commuters squeezed up close to them in the seats and caused them to pause. Sylvia was now looking past the legs of someone who had squeezed a little too much into her space.

"It's gone all postmodern too. Lisa is drawn looking out at the reader saying she needs to escape. I don't like that weird stuff. Don't like her much at all."

They continued the journey in silence for another stop.

Then Greg mumbled, "Tradition is always best in the end."

Sylvia shifted uncomfortably in her seat to let Greg have more room to spread out.

Selfies

It was while sorting through the second set of photos from the third round of printing that I noticed something odd. My wife Maria was busy doing all the things that she enjoys with the kids, you know, feeding and bathing them, while I was sat in the spare room with the latest batch of photos spread out on the bed in front of me.

I can hear the kids downstairs screaming now but Maria is taking care of them while I sort through these photos – each one needs to be labelled and dated before I can file them for future viewing.

I work for a company that does house clearances. You know the kind of thing, your elderly grandmother dies and rather than sort through all the furniture and stuff she had, someone pays you to take it all away and find out if there is anything of value in it. Usually there is nothing, though we have found a few bottles of whisky tucked away behind the best plates in the sideboard.

I always noticed the photographs. I suppose that we are used to photos being something that you store on computers or phones and you assume that when the computer or the phone or you die, they die with you. However, more people than you imagine print their photos and it always annoyed me to find boxes of them with no reference to what they are or when they were taken. I decided to be different.

I must have taken about 3000 photos since the children were born. You know how it is, you visit a park or a museum or a castle or the beach and the first thing that you do is place the children where you want them, take a photo and then upload it to social media for everyone to see. There are still plenty of places that will print them for you and present them in small, blue paper wallets. The second of the latest batch of these (photos 1,550 – 2,000) were spread across the bed.

It was the giraffe that surprised me. Opening one of the packets, the first thing that I saw was a picture of a giraffe. I like giraffes, in fact, they are one of my favourite animals. I always think that it is like a horse was designed by a human committee and then God came along and said 'let's make this one a bit unique'. If you see a photograph of a giraffe up close it has a graceful neck, smoky eyes and real false eyelashes. Maria looks a bit like that - perhaps that is why I married her.

I would have remembered meeting a giraffe, let alone taking a photo of it. We just do not get giraffes in Ross-On-Wye. It must be the lack of high trees. Can you imagine it though? 'How was work today, honey?' 'Bit dull, nothing much happened – oh yes, I was driving down the M50 when a giraffe came along, nothing significant though'.

We had once wanted to take the kids to the safari park at Longleat but they were never going to be ready for a drive down to Wiltshire so we never did. Besides, once I started to look at the next pictures I realised that this was not Wiltshire in the photographs.

The next one was a mud hut – again, not something we have in Ross-On-Wye – and then a group of smiling children in a classroom. The giraffes were against a wide horizon of trees and I recognised none of it. I say none of it, but there was a man with wispy red hair and a toothy smile in some of them. Something about him looked familiar.

"Maria!" I called out but she was not listening, so I decided to go downstairs.

She was standing on the stairs, picking up Lego.

"Hey dear," I said, "something weird is going on with the photos – I've just found a picture of a giraffe."

"When did we see a giraffe?"

"My point exactly! It must be someone else's set of photos."

"We wouldn't want someone else getting our pictures of a day out in Weston-super-Mare, would we?"

I smiled weakly as I thought that she might be trying to make a joke.

"There's something about them …" I started but was not sure what else to say.

I leaned over and ran my hand through Maria's hair affectionately.

"Has anyone ever told you that you look like a giraffe?" I said.

She stared at me strangely so I leaned in and kissed her full on the lips. As I did so, a strange smell hit me full in the nostrils.

"What's that smell?" I asked.

"Eliza was sick on me again."

"You're such a good parent to them," I said and ran my hand through her hair again.

I put the rogue photos aside for the next week and made more progress labelling the others. Each trip to the park, each holiday snap, each moment was carefully documented and filed for future reference. I just could not tear myself away from the giraffe and its friends though.

Maria suggested that I took a break and spent some time with the kids so the next night while she cooked, I sat with them and played. When we ate, she helped Eliza with using a spoon while I pondered where the incorrect photos had come from.

"I phoned the photo shop," I said, "they said that all the photos that they issued to this address were correct. I just can't work it out – I would remember a trip like that."

"Perhaps they're not your memories. Perhaps you should just put them away or put them in the bin and get on with it."

"Maria!" I said with exasperation, "I can't just throw away memories. You know how important this project is to me!"

There was a silence between us while Maria busied herself helping the children to eat.

"They're named after spies, you know," said Maria after a while.

"What? The giraffes?"

"No, your children."

"Our children," I corrected her.

"Are they?"

I looked across the table at Daphne and Eliza and wondered what Maria was talking about. We had agreed that we wanted names that were pretty and feminine and she had suggested both of those.

"Daphne is named after Daphne Park, MI6's top agent in the Congo in the 1960s."

"You said that they were just pretty names."

"I know, I was reading a book on MI6 when Daph came along and thought that it would be good to name her after a strong and successful woman. I didn't think you'd approve."

"Of course, I'd approve!" I replied, "I just don't like it!"

That night we did not speak much more and I retreated to work on the photos again while Maria put the kids to bed and opened a bottle of wine. Later on when she curled up to my back in bed, she whispered –

"Eliza is named after Eliza Manningham-Buller, Director of MI6 in the 2000s."

I pretended to sleep but in my head I was determined to work out when I had taken the mystery photos and why I thought that I recognised the red-haired man.

It turned out that part of the answer came from Gary in the pub. A trip to the pub on a Friday night was still a bit of a ritual in work and I think that I enjoyed it as a chance to have some time away from the children. We all need a break occassionally.

Gary reminded me that a few years ago I had been talking about going on holiday to South Africa. To be honest, it was when we were having a big drinking night in Brannigans and in came some of the girls who work in the call centre opposite. I was talking to this lovely young girl who looked as though she had been poured into her tight jeans and I was trying to impress her. Yes, I know, I had Maria, but it was just a bit of harmless flirting and nothing happened – her friend had a drama in the toilets and she had to go.

However, his comment caught my attention and I thought about it all the way back home on the bus. What if they were photos taken by my camera, but photos taken of a life that I never lived? Imagine if I had not stayed with Maria, imagine if I had got somewhere with that lovely insurance girl and we had gone on safari together (we both liked giraffes, in case you were wondering). Perhaps this is what happens when you have photos developed, but it is normally only the photos of your actual life that are developed.

When I got home, Maria was lying in bed reading. I staggered a little as I came into the bedroom and told her that I had had a revelation. She seemed interested until I mentioned the photos.

"Those bloody photos!" she snapped.

"Have you been drinking?" I slurred, thinking that maybe she had allowed herself a couple of glasses of wine after the children were in bed.

"You need to give up with those damn photos," she repeated and went back to her book.

"No, it's serious, I think that I know what they are!"

I took my clothes off slowly, if a little unsteadily. I tried to put a little wriggle into my movements as I did so because I knew how much Maria liked to watch me getting undressed. She looked over, raised one eyebrow at me, muttered something to herself and then went back to her book.

I climbed next to her under the covers.

"Do you ever think what life would have been like if you had done something different?" I asked.

"Of course," she replied, surprising me somewhat, "everyone does. Had we not done this or that, different paths. What would it have been like if we had never met? But if we had never met, what else would be different? What about – ugh, you smell of beer!"

As she had been talking, I had moved closer to her and tried to plant a big kiss on her lips romantically. I thought that her complaint was a little rich given that she had been smelling of sick the other day. She put her book down by the side of the bed and looked at me directly.

"Yes, I have wondered what it would be like without you, is that the question? But I always think that I would never want to be without our little spies, so this is the best life I could have."

"I love you too," I said with a smile.

I nestled back down under the covers.

"I'll show you some photos from the life I could have led. Tomorrow, though," I promised.

I was actually quite excited about showing Maria the photos. I would not tell her about the insurance girl or anything that might worry her like that but I would tell her that this was the holiday I could have had but which I turned down to be with her. I knew that she would be impressed.

The next day was Saturday and we had a busy day. The sun was out and we went down to the river to feed the ducks and spend some time with the kids. I felt happy and perhaps a little bit closer to Maria having not seen her so much while sorting the photos, but also thinking about how I had made the right choices in life to be where I was now. I took some photos of us all.

That night, once Maria had put the kids to bed, I took her into the spare room and took out the mystery photos. I removed the first one, the picture of the giraffe and passed it to her. I can honestly tell you that her reaction was not what I expected.

At first, she seemed to jump as if the photo had given her a static electricity shock.

"I recognise that giraffe," she said then.

"What do you mean, when have you ever seen a giraffe?" I asked.

"I was there," she said with a sense of wonder creeping into her voice, "I think that I took this photo."

"Don't be daft!" I said, imagining that she had just made a mistake over a trip to the safari park or something but then realising something darker might be happening, "Have you been going out without me?"

"What?"

"I am not sure how to say this Maria but, have you been on holiday without me?"

Maria looked at me with such shock that I knew that I had overstepped the mark. She grabbed a pillow from the bed and hit me with it, not playfully but hard.

"When the hell do I get a holiday? Was that before your younger child was sick on me or after your elder child put her food everywhere except in her mouth?"

"I'm sorry, I'm sorry, I just thought ... how could you?"

I backtracked quickly and she put the pillow back in its place. She was still looking angry, though.

"It makes no sense, I know, but I touch this photo and I have a feeling of having been there."

"Perhaps you saw a documentary?"

Maria grabbed the next one from out of my hands.

"Those children!" she exclaimed, "I know this school too. We were helping there. That's Danielle teaching, she was in our group!"

"What the hell are you talking about?"

Maria was lost in the reminiscences now and was flicking through the photos quickly.

"Yes, we went on the trip with this charity from Newport. Those wide horizons – oh my goodness, I touch these and I am standing there. The heat felt so different and the wind, I can feel the wind on my face."

I snatched some of the photographs back, determined to put a stop to this nonsense.

"You're mad. You've obviously been worn out today."

One photo was left in her hand and she looked down at it. It was then that she looked with horror and then with a kind of longing that I had never seen in her eyes before.

"That's Tim. Oh God, it's Tim. His hair has thinned a little ... well, a lot, but we went together," she said and then running her hand over the photo added, "we left the children with his parents. Trip of a lifetime. A whole month away. God, I felt guilty about leaving the children but ... they loved Tim's parents and we just had to do something."

"The red-haired guy? You know him? He did look familiar!"

"He's my husband," she muttered, "he worried that I was going to have some kind of breakdown and we just ... well, we prepared, but we went. He was frightened of losing me as I was struggling. We had a big talk and he persuaded me that we needed to get away. So we volunteered together and ... and ... these are the photos."

She was standing there in the fading light, running her fingers back and forth over the last photo, smiling at the man in the picture.

"You were married before me?" I asked, now completely dumbfounded.

"No," she said with a smile, "that's Tim Roberts. You met him briefly when we were in college. He had such a crush on me and, to be honest, me on him, but ... well, you were there and ... now here we are."

"Of course," I said, realising that I had never been aware that I had won Maria from the hands of another man.

"Then when did you go on holiday with him?" I asked.

"It wasn't a holiday," she said sternly, "it was a charity expedition to support a local project in South Africa."

"But when?" I demanded.

"In another life," she replied softly, "these are photos from the life that I should have lived."

I'd Do Anything

There is something unsettling about waking up in someone else's house. The light is streaming through the curtains on the wrong side of the room, the glimpse of light behind the door is in the wrong place and you roll over to switch off your alarm clock only to find that it is on the wrong side of the bed.

It took me a few seconds to adjust to being in my brother's house or rather, in his guest bedroom. I remembered where I was, pulled off the sheets and then plodded wearily across the uneven, stone floor to the light switch. I said bedroom but it was really a little annexe across from the main house, a converted outbuilding now providing its own little world for guests to enjoy.

I am not sure why I switched the light on when I could have just opened the curtains. Still, the old flagstones were cold on my feet and I hurriedly jumped back in to the bed. My kid brother had done well for himself. He was the one who had not worked at school, had always been in trouble and had been roundly dismissed by his teachers on Careers Night. Yet, here he was in a big, countryside house with a beautiful family and a guest bedroom with its own ensuite facilities. I was proud of him rather than resentful, though I suppose that I would have been a jealous and grumpy teenager about it had it been twenty years ago.

My life was a million miles away. The actual geography was a lot shorter of course, but back in my flat in Bow I was woken every morning by the number fourteen bus stopping outside my bedroom window and groups of teenage girls playing with their phones while waiting for the school bus. No, it is not awesome that you have set 'Space Unicorn' as your ringtone! Here in Oxfordshire the air was clean, the light was clear and it was the perfect escape for me from reality.

I did not want to disturb anyone in the big house, so I started to wash and dress. I had been thinking of a stroll down by the river, perhaps where Dad used to love walking, when there was an urgent knock at the door. Paul shouted to ask if I was decent and then walked in anyway.

"'Morning, morning," my brother said cheerfully, "did you sleep well?"

"A five star rating for TripAdvisor," I replied, "what is the secret of your success?"

"The secret of my excess is being more handsome, not to mention taller than you," he said with a smile.

It was not true on either count. He was no tall, dark stranger, but a blonde, light-skinned man with a cheeky smile who had always been prone to spots. I had more of our father's darker looks to me and yet ... I was not resentful that he had it all.

"Do you want to see Dad today?" he asked.

That question made me go as cold as the flagstones had been on my feet before I had put my socks on. I am sure that Paul would have seen my face go white too and so he repeated the question. I cleared my thoughts and decided that he must have been asking if I wanted to visit the place in the woods where we had scattered Dad's ashes.

"Why not?" I replied, thinking that Dad always loved the late autumn sunshine and the paths in the woods becoming uneven underfoot with the leaves, so why not.

"Great," said Paul with an enthusiasm that seemed out of place for the morning, "get a move on and come over, Sophia says the kids can't eat until you are there and you know what they're like when they have to wait!"

With that he was gone and I smiled at the thought of all that energy. How did he do it? I leaned over to check the time and realised that the alarm clock was in the wrong place. Whatever time it was, a middle-aged man with three children should not be so chirpy.

I took some clothes from the guest wardrobe and unfolded them gently. It was four years since we lost Dad and we both missed him terribly. I suppose that that was the one time after he had made so much of his life when I saw my brother fall apart. We both loved the man but Paul had spent so much time with him walking in those woods across the river from here that the absence seemed to leave a hole in him that everyone could see.

I fastened the buttons on my shirt and stepped into my shoes. I would probably need walking boots if we were going in the woods later, but I did not want to seem too fussy. I opened the curtains and let the light stream in to the room. Late autumn sunshine, trees across the garden turning to brown ... it was a remarkable view and one that put a spring in your step more than listening to the misfiring engine on the number fourteen.

I opened the door to the bedroom and walked into the hall area outside the guest rooms. Dad was standing there.

* * * * *

What do you say to a dead person when you meet them? Do you hug them? Then again, we were never very big on hugging in my family, even with living people. If there had been no colour in my cheeks before then now I must have looked like a ghost. Oddly, the man in front of me looked full of colour and remarkably healthy.

"Hello son," he said, bringing a smile to my staring face borne of the amusement that he rarely used our names.

I stared at him for a few moments and must have just nodded because he shifted awkwardly on the spot and then continued.

"I suppose that you are a bit surprised," he added, with remarkable understatement.

"Paul said that we could meet you today," I stammered hopelessly.

"Ah yes, sorry to spoil the surprise."

My Dad laughed to himself as he said this and I stared again. He was his recognisable height, he wore his recognisable old jumper (I was always meaning to buy him a replacement) and the only thing missing was the pain of the cancer that had taken him away in that final year.

"You're looking well," I managed, matching him for remarkable understatement.

"I am, son, I am. Look, there'll be time to catch up properly later. You are keeping my grandchildren away from their pancakes if you stay here!"

"Do they know you are here?" I asked.

"Only Paul does right now, that's why he was so excited this morning."

I wanted to tell him that we should not 'talk later when there is time' because there is never enough time. I wanted to tell him that the world was made up of millions of 'we'll talk later' statements that never came true. I wanted to tell him that I had finally bought an old, second-hand piano and put it in my front room in Bow next to the fireplace. I wanted to tell him so much.

He indicated with a hand towards the doorway and I left, trying desperately to think of something that did not sound as trite as 'it's good to see you again'.

* * * * *

Outside, the sun delivered on the early promise glimpsed through the bedroom curtains, but there was a slightly chill wind in the air. The big house was behind the converted outbuilding and the garden sloped away from the house to a river and then some woods beyond. In the middle of the lawn stood a large tree with a swing hanging down from one branch. Those children would marvel one day at how lucky they were to grow up here, I thought.

"Unca! Unca!" shouted Amy as she ran unsteadily across the grass to me.

People with children always imagine that everyone knows their children's ages but the truth is that if you are not caught up in school years and key stages, it is hard to remember. Amy – or Amethyst as she was Christened – was the youngest, not quite yet at school and too young to even remember her grandfather.

Amy took my hand and guided me towards the house. I could see at the back that the French doors were open and that Sophia was setting up breakfast on the table outside. It was possibly the last time of the year when they would be able to do this. Amy was excited for me to see it or possibly just excited about the pancakes.

When I arrived, Sophia stopped from laying out the plates to give me a hug.

"Thank goodness you're here," she said in that slightly more respectable accent than my brother's, "the children were going to mutiny if they had to wait longer!"

We all sat down together. Amy to my left, Emma – that would be Emerald, you see the theme of the naming – her older sister besides her and then across the table was Jeremy who, as a boy, did not have to be named after a jewel. Somewhere along the line though, irony had taken hold and he was now known to the family as 'Jem'.

Jem must have been close to double figures in age now, if not already there, and I gave him a manly nod. He looked like his father, but for bright red hair which would probably mean that he would spend a childhood of being asked if his mother had any 'close male friends' with red hair about nine months before he was born.

"You've seen him, then?" said Paul, who must have been able to tell by my slight unsteadiness that not everything was right.

"Yes," I said, "briefly, but he didn't want to ... err ... he didn't want to delay the breakfast."

Paul simply smiled. I could not believe how calm he was being about this. People do not come back from the dead every day, most especially people who you have loved and mourned.

Sophia and Paul had been to America and fallen in love with American breakfasts. This then was the special treat for the children and, indeed, for themselves on a sunny Saturday morning – sitting out on the paved area behind the house, looking out over that sumptuous garden and eating plates of pancakes topped with maple syrup and cream. It must have been incredibly unhealthy, but the family could enjoy the indulgence together.

Amy tugged my arm throughout, wanting to tell me about her latest toy and I promised to look at it later, her mother having repeatedly told her that she could not leave the table to find it. Emma talked proudly of what she had learned in school about the Battle of Stamford Bridge and summarised her knowledge for us. Jem was quiet and slightly embarrassed by his mother saying how well his schoolwork was going and his father ruffled his hair in an awkward father-son bonding ritual. We never really did hugging in my family.

You can imagine that the small talk of the breakfast table passed over my head somewhat. I woke up a bit when Paul told his wife that he and I would be seeing our father later. She must have presumed like I had done that we would be going over to the woods and so she re-assured him that on a bright autumn day there was plenty to entertain the children. Jem was keen to be the man of the house and mow the lawn, perhaps not realising that his parents had someone that they paid to do that.

As soon as was decent, I made my excuses about brushing my teeth and putting my walking boots on and rushed back across the uneven lawn towards the outbuilding.

* * * * *

"Everyone on social media wants you to spend a particular day grieving," Dad said as he gazed out of the window of the entrance hallway by the guest bedroom, not seeing that I was nodding and agreeing.

"It's like they want you to only grieve on Father's Day or on your birthday or on the day that someone died," I said.

The walls were made of rough, rugged stones that looked like they had kept a stable solid for centuries. Dad ran a hand along one of them and I wondered about whether he could feel them, being that he was dead and all.

I realised that he was looking at his grandchildren playing by the tree. Emma was on the swing, Amy was rushing around it excitedly and Jem was pushing the mower down towards the river with a look of pride, the long, orange electrical cable snaking behind him through the grass to the house.

"Amethyst is only here due to me, you know," he said slightly sheepishly, turning to look at me again.

"What do you mean?"

"Your brother – I know this is hard to imagine but think about how I feel – he and Sophia, they were missing from the funeral preparations for about twenty minutes, weren't they? He just felt like he wanted to and although she thought it was disrespectful, they ... and well, who takes condoms to a funeral?"

My mouth must have fallen open a little as he told me this. Dad laughed at the sight.

"He told me, before you ask," he continued, "I don't think that I wanted to hear that either, but it's nice to know that Amethyst owes her existence to some irresponsible mourning!"

Dad moved away from the window towards a deep, enamel basin which was on the other side of the room, perhaps a leftover from when this was a farm building. I still had no words so he continued speaking.

"He always was the irresponsible one. He grieved a lot too. Did you know that he was off work for nearly a year?"

"I knew that he missed a lot of work, but I ..."

"Had counselling, they burnt through Sophia's savings to keep afloat. It was very tough for them."

Dad turned on the tap above the basin and seemed amused that water came out. He washed his hands in the cold stream. I was still struggling to speak in response to all this new information. How long had he been around? He seemed to have had a lot of information from Paul – had he been living in these outbuildings, sleeping in the same bed that I had slept in?

"I mourned too!" I said with a hint of childish protest, as if I were complaining that Paul always got more sweets than me (he always did).

Dad gave me a re-assuring smile and a wave of a wet hand as if to say that he understood. I felt annoyed though and carried on speaking, even though he turned back to the sink.

"I was devastated when we lost you. I knew that the cancer would win in the end but, all the same. It is always too soon, you must know that from when you lost your own parents. I was devastated. Okay, so I did my job and never talked to a professional about it, but I missed you. I mourned. I spent days wanting to put posts on social media just saying that I missed you but knowing that everyone would think that it was time to move on!"

My words came out in an uncontrollable flow, rather like the tap and as he nodded to them, Dad turned off the tap and turned back to face me. He looked around for a towel and then started to shake his hands dry in an inefficient manner.

"You got over it though, didn't you?" he said, "Or rather, you learned to live without me around. That's the difference between you and Paul. You would like to talk to me about things, but you accept that I have gone and that you have to accept that. Paul doesn't. Paul wants me back every day."

I still felt as though this was a previously forgotten rivalry being stoked and that I was being judged for not mourning enough. Yet, I could understand Dad's point. I had accepted that he had died. I had known him and loved him and now I missed him, but I knew that I was never going to see him again. That is, except at that moment, which may have been why Paul was so much more relaxed about this than me.

I opened the door into the bedroom and sat on the bed. The light from the window was making a four-sided shape across the floor and I realised that I had left the light on earlier. I shook my head.

"You mentioned social media," I said, knowing that my father was never a fan of it, "it's like those daft posts that say 'if you see a robin then it means someone who has died is looking after you'. It's such offensive nonsense! It just means that there is a robin in your garden!"

Dad chuckled and walked over to sit near me on the bed. Note, not next to me, we were not a physically close family in hugging or personal body space either.

"That's the thing," he agreed, "all those Facebook posts saying 'I'd give anything to see Dad again' but would they? Would they really? Your brother would, he would 'Like' one of those posts in a heartbeat but not you. You would not give anything."

I looked at him, at those kindly features that had laughed at jokes I made that were not funny, who had wished me well when I moved to London with the only money he could spare stuffed into my pocket, who had comforted and re-assured me and I so wanted to tell him that I would do anything to see him again. It seemed to be what our society told me that I should do. He was right though, I accepted that he was gone and that that was how things were.

I stood up and walked away from him because I needed some space to put these thoughts into words, words that I would not find cruel or unpleasant to the man who I had loved more than anyone.

"You wouldn't give anything to see me again," repeated my Dad, "but your brother would."

I was about to speak when there was a loud sound from out across the lawn. Then there was shrieking and I instantly panicked. I could not see what was going on but I knew that something was wrong.

I ran to the door and saw a distant scene across the lawn. Paul holding two shrieking girls to him while their mother ran out of the house, screaming. There on the lawn in front of them was a ginger-haired boy lying flat out next to where the lawnmower had run over its electric cable.

I rushed out of the door and then stopped. I was about to turn around to say something to Dad but then I thought that he was right. I would not give anything to see him again.

Freaky Tuesday

"Muuuuuum!" said Efanie, rolling her eyes and pouting.

Efanie's mother ignored her daughter's protests and continued speaking to the doctor.

"She doesn't want me to mention it, but it was her college who sent us here," she said.

"Ah yes," replied Dr Latimer, tapping a pencil against her face calmly as if it would show that she was listening and thinking, "I saw that there have been problems with Efanie's behaviour and attendance."

"I am in the room, y'know!" said Efanie, waving at the doctor, "And, by the way, I am sixteen, I don't need my mother to come to the doctor's with me!"

"I'm sorry," replied Dr Latimer, "it is occasional that I have referrals from the college and your mother did insist that she attended. It may actually help with what I am thinking about proposing. Have you not been attending your classes?"

Efanie looked away and stared up at the ceiling, hoping that it would not look too defensive a posture, though she was pleased that the doctor was finally paying attention to her.

"I just have **so** much going on, right now. College, it's not just about the studying, it's like the whole experience. That's why we pay for education, isn't it?" she said eventually.

Mrs Baxter looked over at her daughter and thought for a moment that she might flip her black hoodie over her head, her standard way of avoiding conversation with her parents. However, Efanie had stopped speaking and was now just sulking and staring.

Dr Latimer stood up and started to walk around her small office slowly. There was not much room with a desk, a bookcase, two chairs and two other people in there, but she wanted to give the impression of great thought. She was going to suggest something to them that they might not quite believe and she felt that it would need some build up.

"You're not incorrect," she said, once she had reached a position behind the Baxters.

"There!" said Mrs Baxter, lapsing back into point-scoring in a way that suited the role of teenage daughter more than the role of middle-aged mother.

"Actually, I was agreeing with Efanie."

That comment made Mrs Baxter swing around and look at the doctor. Who was she anyway? What qualifications did she have? Why had the college sent them to her? Why did she not lose some weight if she was going to advise people on their lifestyles?

Dr Latimer could feel the resentment coming from Mrs Baxter, so she simply removed her glasses and spoke, safe in the knowledge that she could not see the growing indignation that she expected.

"We always say that when a teenager is late for school or college, what is wrong with them? We never ask what is wrong with the college. If education was made to be an experience that excited and interested the student, maybe more of them would turn up ..."

"Oh, don't give me that new age talk, I was never like that at her age," snapped Mrs Baxter, "I have another daughter too - Megan - only in Primary now but she is not a problem."

Dr Latimer walked back to her desk slowly. This meant walking around Mrs Baxter, which she did carefully without making contact with her, either physical contact or eye contact.

"Trouble is, we don't seem to realise that teenagers are different creatures. It's amazing how quickly we forget what it is like - I have met 20 year olds who have completely forgotten what being sixteen is like. You know, they have done experiments where teenagers and adults are hooked up to MRI scanners and their brainwaves checked."

By now Dr Latimer had reached her chair and she sat down heavily. It was one of those black leather chairs that is supposed to indicate who is in charge, though on this occasion it simply let out an audible sigh as she returned to her place.

"I don't know about all that," said Mrs Baxter, "but Alan - my husband - and I have tried everything ..."

Dr Latimer lifted up a hand to indicate that she had not stopped speaking.

"While hooked up to the MRI scanners, they showed teenagers and adults things associated with rewards and things associated with punishments."

"They reacted differently, I suppose," interrupted Mrs Baxter, who was finding the doctor's laborious phrasing annoying by this stage.

"Not just a little. Not just a bit. Completely off the charts. We ask teenagers to behave sensibly but they simply don't have the ability to react like we do. Did you know that the human brain does not finish forming until the early twenties? Impulse control, consequences, planning for the future - teenagers simply do not have that part of the brain that does all these things yet. When we punish them for not behaving like adults, we punish them for not being something that it is impossible for them to be."

Dr Latimer finished this speech by picking up her pencil and prodding the blunt end against her cheek. She never used a pencil for anything other than emphasising a point, but it was very good for that.

Efanie was looking at her mother with confused triumph. She knew that she had been referred to as not quite a human being, but she also felt as though Dr Latimer was on her side and there were only two sides for Efanie. Most of the world seemed to be on the other side, the side that was against her.

"You think that I should just give up, then?" asked Mrs Baxter, after taking a moment to think about this, "Girls will be girls or some nonsense. I don't think that you appreciate how hard it is at the moment and I ... I do want the best for her."

Mrs Baxter looked over at her daughter as she said these last words and if Efanie was sceptical about their meaning, Dr Latimer did sympathise.

"I can offer you something ... something a little different, if you really want to see how your daughter sees the world," replied Dr Latimer.

Efanie snorted contemptuously. Unfortunately, the effort of doing so dislodged a long, curly strand of blonde hair, which fell over her face.

"While researching this, we managed to find a way to temporarily reverse the process of adulthood ..."

"What? No-one's experimenting on me!" shouted Efanie, standing up to hopefully emphasise her point.

"Not you, your mother."

"Why, you can't mean ... experiments?" asked Mrs Baxter calmly.

"It's very simple. When looking at the reaction in the brain, we worked out how to reverse it so that - only temporarily - an adult reaction could be as extreme as a teenage reaction. We also worked out how to temporarily reduce the signals from the areas of the brain which form last. It's been a fascinating experience."

"What is this, some kind of 'Freaky Friday' nonsense?" asked Mrs Baxter.

"Freaky what?" asked Efanie.

"It was a film," explained the doctor, "mother and daughter swapped bodies. Came to understand each other yadda yadda yadda."

"Don't want any of her life!" muttered Efanie.

Dr Latimer shook her head. These two might not have been the people to explain this to after all.

"No, not actually swap bodies, that is obviously impossible and ... also not a very good film really ... all a bit trite and obvious and ..."

Mrs Baxter was scowling at the doctor as if to ask if they had turned up to this appointment for a film review or a medical consultation.

"Ah yes, sorry, sorry, where was I? Err ... we could give you the chance to experience your daughter's reactions to the world for a week or so. No body swap nonsense, just like ... I don't know ... like being drunk I suppose, temporarily you would feel different about the world."

"And she gets to be me?" asked Mrs Baxter.

"No chance!" snorted her daughter.

"No chance indeed. We have not done that to date, it would be only you we would work with. However, some people have found it very useful. That's the problem, most adults can't cope with thinking like a teenager."

"You're kidding me! Sitting on your fat arse, having nothing but free time and no responsibilities? How hard is that?"

"You think that's my life? You understand nothing! Nothing!" shouted Efanie, storming out of the office, her black hood flipped up over her curls as she did so.

The two adult women remained in the room, staring at each other in silence for a while.

"Are you going to go after her?" asked Dr Latimer.

"We're miles from home, she won't walk. She'll be sitting on the car. I want to prove her wrong, if that's okay, doctor."

"Call me Kate."

"Sylvia," replied Sylvia Baxter, "That one's going to be mocking me all the way home but I'll show her that I can live her easy little life. How hard can it be?"

"We do find most parents have forgotten how hard it is and ..."

However, there was no point Dr Latimer continuing as Sylvia Baxter was already out of the door. Instead, the doctor stood up and looked at the medical certificate hanging on her office wall. One day they would recognise this as a ground-breaking procedure. There was just that one nagging question that dogged everything.

She wrote 'Sylvia & Efanie' on to her calendar.

* * * * *

"Careful now," said Dr Latimer as she held Sylvia's arms to balance her as she tried to get up, "take it slowly."

Sylvia Baxter glanced around the hospital room and then sat up slowly. She was faintly aware of having been drugged and having been unconscious but rather like waking from an intense dream, she was having difficulty finding the 'normal' setting on her world.

"Listen to me, this is important," said the doctor, in a tone of voice that annoyed Sylvia straight way, "you are going to find this hard to adjust to. It's kind of like doing puberty all in one go. It's only temporary, but watch out. Look both ways before crossing the road, for one."

"What?" said Sylvia, batting away one of the doctor's arms and looking around for her coat. Ah yes, she remembered now, she had come to the hospital in a long, floral dress to look sophisticated. That was a weird thing to do for a medical procedure, she thought.

"You will find your head whirring with thoughts initially. A lot of things will be heightened but remember that your grasp of consequences is shut off. You are most likely to walk out of here and step into the road without looking to see if there is any traffic coming."

"What are you, my mother?" asked Sylvia incredulously at the woman who looked no more than a few years older than her.

"Car accidents - been a lot of them out there. Adults suddenly thinking they're invincible or rather, not realising the consequences of not looking both ways when they step out into the road."

"I feel good," announced Sylvia and she did, she felt kind of alive and interested and excited by the world around her.

Why was she wasting time in the hospital, she wanted to go out there and experience the world! Why was this doctor holding her back? Sylvia batted the doctor's other arm away and rose steadily to her feet.

"Just go easy and remember it's part of an experiment," said Dr Latimer slowly.

"Yeah, sure, really hungry," said Sylvia.

With that, she signed several pages of release and indemnity forms without reading them and wandered out into the bright, bright sunshine of a June day. What was she going to do now?

She took a step forwards and a taxi sounded its horn at her angrily.

"Watch where you're going!" Sylvia shouted as she jumped back on to the pavement.

* * * * *

"Mum, are you all right?" asked Efanie when her mother returned to the house later that day.

"Yes fine," replied Sylvia, "what's for dinner?"

Mr Baxter stuck his head out from the kitchen and shouted 'home made pizzas' to a cheer from Efanie. Then he added, "It'll be another half an hour mind you, I've had to do Meggie's food first."

"I'd better have a snack then," said Sylvia, but she was looking at her husband in a way that was feeling weird.

"A snack!" said Alan, "it's only half an hour, honest."

Sylvia walked past him while eyeing him up and down. OMG, he was hot. How had she not noticed? Yes, there was a five year old in the kitchen running around and the larger child who was sitting on the sofa trying to straighten her hair had been around forever, but how had she noticed in all that time how hot Alan was?

Sylvia picked up a biscuit from a box leftover from their last house party. Alan reached out and smacked her on the wrist gently and playfully. Wow! It was like a bolt of electricity through her body. The touch of his hand was incredible, kind of familiar but also kind of exhilarating. She wanted him there and then. Over the kitchen table. On the sofa. Anywhere. She wanted him and did not want to wait.

"I told you, pizzas are on their way. Just have some patience. Half an hour," he said insistently.

"That's ages," she complained. nibbling on a biscuit in what she hoped was a seductive manner.

"Get a plate then, the crumbs will go everywhere."

How could a man who was so hot be such a killjoy? Or was it her? Suddenly Sylvia was hit by a wave of self-doubt. Had she upset him by wanting a biscuit? Was he annoyed with her? How could she tell? Would he still love her? She wanted to find her phone so she could message one of her friends to ask. Someone on the internet must know.

Sylvia walked into the sitting room and sat down in an armchair, pondering these points.

"Mum, are you all right?" repeated Efanie.

"You wouldn't understand," said her mother and reached for her phone.

* * * * *

The pizzas were eaten and Alan watched over Efanie as she completed her college work. Sylvia was watching Alan. Okay, so he was mostly bald now and his beard hardly compensated in the way that he had hoped, but he was so kind and giving. He asked if she was all right and it sounded so sexy and so loving. This really was the man that she was going to be with for evermore. She felt an urge to sign her name as 'Mrs Baxter' over and over again to remind herself. She also felt that same urge to just feel his touch on her. She wanted the children to go away so she could be alone with him.

Efanie spent longer on her supervised homework session than she wanted to do but her father eventually let her go to her bedroom to message her friends, complaining about how unfair it was and how her mother was behaving oddly.

Sylvia went up to the bedroom slightly before her husband and started to hunt through a drawer in her dresser frantically. Surely there must be something suitable here, she thought? Then she found something, a short, silk, black nightie which had been tucked under her pyjamas for several years. If it would still fit, then it would be just fine.

Luckily it did fit and she felt it hover around her and roll down to the right point just above the knee. She tried to adopt a position stood with one leg up on the bed but it was a little unsteady. She threw her hair back over one shoulder. Then she tried the other shoulder. Sylvia put out a hand to balance herself against the wardrobe. Alan was taking a long time in the bathroom.

Finally the bedroom door opened and her husband walked in, not looking at her but idly flossing with a toothpick.

"I think that we might be getting there with our teenager," he was saying, "you know what the doctor told you about having extreme reactions ..."

Alan's voice trailled off at this point because he had looked up and noticed his wife. She smiled at him in a way that she thought would seem seductive. Initially it made him lose concentration and stab one of his gums with the toothpick. Then he jumped back and slammed the door for fear that someone else might see her.

"Do you like what you see?" she asked him.

"Yes, but ... it's Monday night," was all that he could manage.

"I know," she said, bending down and climbing under the duvet cover, "but why can't we have some fun. I've been watching you all night and fancying you and I want to do something about it. Don't you?"

"Well, of course," said Alan carefully, taking off his shirt and replacing it with his pyjama top, "but we have work and college day tomorrow. You need to take Megan to school and then hop over to work. We're going to need all the energy we can get."

By now Alan had removed his work trousers and folded them neatly on a chair. He had replaced them with his pyjama trousers, the whole process achieved one garment at a time so that he was never naked, as was his habit. He climbed under the duvet next to his wife.

"They get all our energy, it's not fair," she said, running a hand between his pyjama buttons and across his chest, "why don't we do something for ourselves tonight?"

"Well, of course, I'd like to, but we have to think of the children and the need to show a ... what are you doing?"

Sylvia had started to slide down under the bedclothes. Her head poked out from under the duvet to reply to him.

"Do you remember when we stayed in that hotel in Covent Garden? Do you remember what I did to you that night?" she asked.

"Yes, but that was twenty years ago and frankly ..."

However, Alan never finished his sentence because his wife's head had disappeared under the covers and he was feeling persuaded that it might just be worth risking a little tiredness at work the next day to recreate that hotel visit from long ago.

In the next room, Efanie had been awake listening to music and messaging her friends when she heard odd sounds from the room next door. At first, she ignored them but as they seemed to be getting louder, she climbed in to her bed and tried to bury her head under the covers. She swore and stuck her head under the pillow in disgust.

* * * * *

The alarm clock sounded its dull call through the morning air and both Alan and Sylvia woke up. However, whereas Alan turned to switch it off, Sylvia rolled on to his chest and asked if they could not just press snooze and have a bit longer.

"No, come on, we have to be up or the kids won't get up. You're taking Megan in to school, remember?" he said.

"What? No-one told me! What am I going to wear?" said his wife, sitting up in bed suddenly.

"We talked about it yesterday. You were going to sort out your clothes before we went to bed," said Alan calmly.

"Yes but, I didn't have a chance, I was distracted - you distracted me. It's not my fault. Oh hell, what am I going to do?"

Alan shook his head. He did remember something of this from when they first met in their late teens.

"Well, the headteacher said no pyjamas or dressing gowns so I am going to say that anything else is fine."

"You idiot!" muttered his wife as she opened the wardrobe and started to sort through clothes, "Laura will be there. Carrie too. Daisy will have her cameraphone no doubt ..."

"And ... so?"

"So? So! If I don't look perfect, they'll be messaging and photo'ing around the Mums group before I have even dropped Megan off!"

"Yes, but what I mean is, does it really matter what they think?"

Sylvia turned around from the wardrobe and glared at her husband with such intensity that he felt as though it was pushing him off the bed. He tried to smile and re-assured her that he would make sure that the children were fed, dressed and ready by the time that she was ready.

Sure enough, with only a small amount of drama and a brief argument about use of the bathroom in the morning, Efanie was dispatched towards college, Alan left for work and Sylvia was left to take Megan to the trial which was arrival at the school gates. Sylvia thought that something quite stylish but also casual was going to be the answer. She wanted to rock the 'oh this, oh I only wear this to come to the school' look. She could do it.

When she arrived at the school gates, Laura was wearing a bright purple scarf that she had not seen before. Otherwise, her usual group seemed reasonably on usual trends and she did not have to worry too much. Sylvia wished Megan well for the day and then said hello to the other mothers as her daughter ran off.

"How are you girls, what's the gossip?" she asked brightly.

"You're later than normal," observed Laura rather archly.

"Feeling the strain of working and parenting?" asked Carrie, who had always disapproved of Sylvia going back to work.

"No," said Sylvia proudly, "I've been up all night shagging."

Laura, Carrie and Daisy simply stared at her and wondered if they had misheard her.

"Too much information!" said Laura with a hand raised as if it could block words reaching her ears.

"What?" said Sylvia, "Don't you believe me?"

"Definitely too much information!" repeated Laura.

"More to the point," asked Daisy, with a cutting edge to her voice, "what is your husband going to do when he finds out about this?"

There was laughter from all of them and Sylvia felt stung. She was just trying to fit in. Then again, she was alone. That was the thing, when she looked around her life, she simply did not fit in here, work, home, she was born as someone who did not have a place in the world. No-one else was going to understand that.

"Don't you work on a Tuesday anyway?" asked Carrie.

Work? Oh yes, Sylvia remembered her part-time job on the other side of the city. How the hell was she going to get there? How was she going to get home and change and get there in time? Why had no-one told her about this? Why was she expected to do everything?

She phoned Alan. He could come and pick her up and take her there.

* * * * *

It was the end of the work and school day and Sylvia Baxter sat in the bath with the shower above her raining a torrent down on the top of her head. From here it divided into two rivers, one down the back of her body and into the narrow crevice between her back and the edge of the bath and the second down her face, on to her breasts, stomach and into the bath below. Sylvia was barely paying attention to whether the water went in her eyes or in her mouth or made a meandering motion across her stomach. Sylvia felt that everything was ruined.

It had been a bad day. The altercation at the school gates had been a disaster. An e-mail had arrived later that day from the Parent Teacher Association that they were worried that she was a bad influence on the children involved in the group. There were accusations from one parent that she had talked about obscene things within the school grounds, within earshot of children, with unthinkable consequences.

Sylvia had also been late for her job and though Alan was a calm and kindly man, she could tell that he was losing patience with her. He had not been happy being called out of work and transporting her across the city. He was solidly blaming the time that she had spent selecting an outfit, but he simply did not understand the pressure that she was under. No-one understood.

Back home she had wanted to fire off an angry 'screw you!' e-mail to the PTA but after joking about it with Efanie, her own daughter decided that it was perhaps going a little bit far and perhaps she should not send an angry response after all. No-one understood.

Sylvia had once seen a cartoon that felt a lot like this. It was of a woman standing under a showerhead with her own head bowed and instead of water, the shower produced judgements. You are not good enough, you are ugly, no-one will ever love you and so on. This was how Sylvia felt. She was a failure as a wife and a mother, no-one loved her, she was alone, everything in her life was wrong, she was fat and ugly and had not lost her baby weight let alone addressed her thigh gap problem. Everything around her told her that she would never get anywhere, be anything or do anything and her self-confidence felt like no more than the echo of a sound that she had heard a long time ago.

Sylvia cried and the tears mixed with the water that fell on her breasts. Her breasts were the wrong shape. She could see folds of fat beneath them. No wonder no-one liked her. She was never going to be popular. She had failed the children by going back to work. She had failed the children because of the time that she spent at home with them. No wonder Efanie was failing at college.

Sylvia looked up into the showerhead and thought of all those failures and all those judgements washing down on to her and drowning her. How was she ever going to do anything with her life when she could barely breathe under all this water?

She looked over to the sink and thought that she might as well shave her legs. It was something dull and functional that not even a loser like her could possibly do wrongly. However, as she leaned over to reach her razors, she realised that there was a pack of unused razor blades for Alan's razor. He liked using sharp blades for his beard and seeing them, Sylvia had a terrible idea. She picked one up and sat back down in the bath.

The shower was loud enough to hide any sound. Slowly she drew the razor across her left leg. Oh, she heard herself say to no-one in particular, I cut myself shaving, it is nothing. It was only a scratch though and so she drew it back, pushing harder until with a suppressed ouch and bit lip, she drew blood. She hated herself for admitting this, but there was something of a relief to it. Not a pleasure so much as a thankfulness that she could still feel something. The drops of blood and the wound that stung against the bathwater were a reminder that she was alive. She moved to the other leg - two accidents shaving were hardly going to cause comment?

Sylvia took a deep breath and pulled the razor away. This was stupid. She could not let this feeling overwhelm her. Then again, who would notice ...

"Mum? Are you all right?" shouted Efanie through the door.

Bless her, thought Sylvia, my very own messed-up teen is stopping me self-harming. That is what this is, something I had only read about in the newspapers and wondered why the hell anyone would do it. Sylvia smiled through her tears and let out a big sigh.

"Yes dear, I'm fine. I'm fine," she replied.

She wanted to call her an angel or thank her somehow for interrupting her. She wanted to re-assure her that she was loved and that she did not ever have to worry or be insecure about her family caring about her.

"Good, 'cos you're taking bloody ages in there. Get a move on and stop being so selfish!" came the reply.

* * * * *

"Dad!" said Efanie, as she wandered into her parents' bedroom without pausing to be invited in.

Alan Baxter was laying out papers on the bed. Before Megan was born, he had had a little study across the landing, but now that was a nursery. He did not like doing work in the bedroom, but it seemed like the only free space for papers sometimes. At least, it was space for papers until Efanie pushed them out of the way and sat next to him. Alan put his arm around her protectively.

It was a warm day and she was only wearing a t-shirt and jeans and his arm fitted around her neatly. He sighed and wished that she would have a growth spurt, he was sure that her round figure was not making her popular at college. Then again, perhaps they could persuade her to eat square meals instead of endless sugary drinks and sweets. However, he also knew that they had had that conversation many times and it had never ended with a successful conclusion - his measure of success being that she would agree with him.

"What's wrong Number One Daughter?" he asked instead.

"I'm ... I'm worried about Mum, Dad."

Efanie pulled her head from out of underneath his arm and looked at him to see if he was taking her seriously. Alan nodded and so Efanie continued.

"I'm serious, Dad. You've been doing so much in the last few days. You've been cooking, I've seen you cleaning up and stuff. Mum's not helping you with anything."

"A bit like you?" said her father, with a wry smile.

"Don't be silly, I've got far too much on at the moment. No, I mean the stuff that you two do for ... you know ... you know, the stuff that it's your job to do."

Alan laughed and put an arm out to his daughter again, but she looked out of the window instead.

"Your Mum will be fine, it's just this strange experiment. I'm enjoying cooking for you all every night."

"Yeah, well," said Efanie, looking around the room, before adding, "it's like I have to remind her of things. She forgets what we're supposed to be doing the next day and stuff. It's annoying."

Alan looked at his daughter as she pouted and then brought out her phone from her pocket. He noticed something new.

"When did you break the screen on your phone?" he asked.

"Oh that, oh, I threw it at Sophie Morris. I had to, right, because she was moving in on Pete. She has to know where she stands ... and that should be nowhere near Pete."

"How are you going to afford to get that repaired?" asked Mr Baxter.

"Dunno."

"Didn't you think about that before you threw it?"

"Oh shut up, Dad. I'm worried about Mum, that's all."

Alan reached over and this time Efanie did not move away from the half-hug completely. She let her father tell her that things would be okay. Then she felt him laugh to himself.

"Do you think that's what it's all about? Maybe if we gave you more responsibility and stopped trying to tell you what to do, then you would have become more mature about things? Perhaps if we were a little irresponsible instead of always trying to be the all-knowing, sensible adults ..."

Efanie slid down off the bed to her feet and turned to face her father. She felt awkward having this conversation and nervously her right hand scratched her left upper arm. This caused the short sleeve of her t-shirt to lift slightly and her father noticed some white lines marked across her skin. He had never noticed those before, he thought, they must have come from a growth spurt a few years ago, though he thought that she had been the same height for some years.

Efanie walked to the door, shaking her head.

"I will be glad when it is all over," she said, "I just want everything to go back to normal."

* * * * *

"Al! Al! Al!" shouted Sylvia, suddenly throwing her arms around her husband.

He was trying to pull on his trousers as she did this and it caused him to fall over backwards on to the bed, with his wife wrapped around his legs.

"I have to go to work and if that's what you're after ..." he started.

"No," she said, "what if I'm pregnant?"

"What?"

Sylvia grabbed a pillow and hit him with it slightly too hard and he pushed her off.

"Sorry," he said, "it's unlikely, but ... why would you be ... well, I know what causes it ... err ..."

Alan sighed and silently gave thanks that the experiment was nearly over. He could see the advantages to someone gaining an insight into how teenagers think but when you were forced to be around them, it became tiring. He was a cautious middle-aged man now and he wanted his cautious wife back. He hugged her gently.

"If you were, then we would raise a third child. It was only five years ago we last went through this, we could do it again. However, if you're not then you're not. And why do you think that you are?"

"Sorry," said his wife quietly, "I just suddenly panicked and didn't really think."

At that moment, the door to their bedroom flung open and there was Efanie ready for college and looking at them expectantly.

"I thought you were driving me to college today!" she demanded.

"Don't you ever knock?" said her mother grumpily.

"Efanie," said Mr Baxter with pride, "we think that you mother may be pregnant."

"Ew! Gross!" shouted Efanie and stormed off down the stairs.

"Knew that would get rid of her," said Alan with a smile.

* * * * *

Sylvia Baxter lay down in the hospital bed carefully. Dr Latimer was busy checking on drug measurements and it was as she watched her work that Sylvia felt that she wanted a few answers.

"How often do you do this?"

Dr Latimer paused and sighed. She looked as though she was struggling with the answer to a question that she had been asked before.

"Let me put it this way," she said, "how did you find the experience?"

"Well ... honestly ... especially now it's wearing off, both kind of brilliant and also kind of scary. I see about that constant up and down, that exhilaration and that boredom mixed together. It's ... yes, I admit, it's tough for them. It doesn't excuse not going to college and ..."

Sylvia stopped because Dr Latimer was smiling at her.

"It is wearing off, I see," she said, "but we will do a few tests with you and give you all the required antidotes. Then we'll do an MRI to confirm that your responses are back to ..."

Sylvia's face went from one of quiet contentment in having proved her daughter wrong to one of realisation. She knew exactly why this technology had not been rolled out and the question that no-one could answer.

"Normal?" she whispered.

"Yes," said Dr Latimer, softly, "but what are you asking yourself now?"

"Maybe," stammered Sylvia, "maybe ... it's the teenagers who are the ones who are reacting normally and we're the ones who've got it wrong."

Dr Latimer nodded and then pushed the stretcher into the MRI scanner. That was the question no-one would answer. What if it was the teenagers who were the normal human beings?

The Dating Questionnaire

A few years ago, my life was affected by a sudden influx of Rebeccas. There was Rebecca the Cinema-Goer, Rebecca Tonteg, Artistic Rebecca and, of course, Rebecca Who Shall Never Be Mentioned Again And I Think That We Can All Agree That That Is Sensible (or Rebecca WSNBMAAITTWCAATTIS ... for short).

Shortly before my second date with Rebecca the Cinema-Goer, I was talking to a friend about this. I like second dates. First dates are all about nerves and uncertainty. Second dates are the point where I can relax and be more 'myself' with someone. That's probably why I don't get any third dates.

I said this to my friend who said that she thought that I was a decent guy but then again, she only knew me as a friend and I might be a nightmare to date. I realised that this was an important question – am I a nightmare to date? How would I answer this question? I realised that I needed to do some research. That's why I invented the Dating Questionnaire. This would be sent to all ex-girlfriends or women who I had dated and through their responses I could discover if I was a nightmare to date.

The Dating Questionnaire

Please answer the following questions as honestly as possible. Your details will be kept for monitoring and research purposes only, including for songs, short stories, novellas, novels, blogs, Notes, research papers and angry post-it notes.

Question One : Please state your name and age.

Question Two : How long did we date or were we in a relationship for?

Supplementary question : Would we agree on the date when the relationship ended?

Please explain your answer in less than 50 words but more than 2 words (drawings are not allowed).

Question Three : Why did our relationship end? Was it because –

(a) You slept with my best friend
(b) You slept with one or more of my other friends
(c) Some other error that you made during the course of the relationship

There is no other answer available for this question.

Question Four : Included with this questionnaire are four drawings of activities we may have undertaken during our relationship. Please rate these on a scale from '1' for 'Enjoyable' to '5' for 'Pleasurable'. Please note that due to a printing error, picture three is upside down.

Question Five : Would you recommend our relationship to a friend?

Question Six : Your favourite time spent together with me was -

(a) On holiday
(b) On holiday and on day trips
(c) On holiday and on day trips and weekends
(d) On holiday and on day trips and weekends and week days
(e) All of the above

Question Seven : Since dating me has your self-confidence about your looks improved to the point where you could now get a job as –

(a) An actress
(b) A hand model
(c) A foot model
(d) A hand and foot model
(e) A body double
(f) A body double but only for yourself

Question Eight : Since we broke up, how would you describe the degree to which you miss me?

(a) I find it hard to carry on without you and life is only just bearable
(b) I have compromised with life because I know that I will never find anyone else as wonderful as you
(c) I realise that when I dumped you I threw away my greatness chance of happiness. It is my burden to live with this regret.
(d) Not at all

If you answered (d) Not at all, then please answer the following supplementary question –

Supplementary question :

Are you crazy?

    Answer (a) Yes

    Answer (b) Yes

Thank you for taking part in this questionnaire. Please return it by e-mail or post to the address on the reverse of this form. Your co-operation is appreciated.

* * * * *

It worked. Six months later, I had not received a single response. This could only mean that I was not a nightmare to date, surely?

There are no answers available to this question.

Big Decisions

(1)

"Sorry I'm running a bit late," said Mary Davies as she put her briefcase down on the table and smiled at the couple who had reached the pub before her.

"I'm Gerry," said the man, shaking her hand, "it's okay, we ate already."

"And I'm Estelle, but please call me Elle," said the woman, also shaking her hand, "the halloumi and mushroom burger is particularly good."

"Gerry, Elle, thank you for meeting me here. It's our new initiative – get out into the community and meet people rather than insist you come to us. Are you local?"

Mary started to unpack her briefcase on to the pub table and pile sets of documents around the plates and condiments.

"About ten miles down the road," replied Gerry, "we didn't even know this pub was here. Strange really, small village with a big pub."

"Ah, *Yr Hen Alarch*," said Mary, "there's quite a few villages around here so I suppose that people come to this one. Like a Park & Ride station, only it's Drink & Sit. This back bar used to be an under 25s bar – well, I'm told, you can imagine it's over forty years since I was on big nights out. But, it's a lot nicer as a restaurant, I think. Do you speak Welsh?"

As she spoke, Mary settled across the table from Gerry and Elle and they watched as she shut her briefcase again and smiled at them. She had everything in place and was ready to advise them.

"Err ... no," said Elle, remembering the question, "we've always wanted to learn but, you know, time ..."

Mary wrote on her notepad 'Gerard (male) & Estelle (female)'. Underneath that she wrote 'not Welsh speakers'.

Elle had been the more reluctant of the two to meet a mortgage broker in the back of a pub, but Gerry had insisted that it was the only way to do it close to home. Mary gave her confidence though. She exuded calm, she had a briefcase and she must have been around sixty and therefore must have had several mortgages herself. Elle trusted her. Gerry looked at Mary a little more suspiciously. These were big decisions that they had to make and he wanted the right person to be asking the questions.

"Battered gherkins?" asked a waiter who had been hovering near the table since Mary came in.

"I beg your pardon?" asked Mary.

"Well Madam, I really meant your young friends here. Many people match a burger with our battered gherkins. They are served with a thousand island dressing and are quite a speciality in the locality ..."

"Sorry, but we have more important decisions to make than about battered gherkins," interrupted Gerry.

"If you insist, Sir."

"But I'll have a soda water with a dash of lime, please," said Mary, catching the young man's arm before he turned away, "I do like these country pubs. The wooden beams, the poky little bars, real fires, the way the front door opens straight out on to the narrow street, it's the feel of them ..."

Mary realised that her two customers were only nodding out of politeness so she moved to business.

"This is my card and the details for Garvey & Garvey," she said, "if you ever have a complaint then you can call that number. However, our aim is to get you the best mortgage possible. What is it you are looking for?"

Gerry took the lead and explained that when they had bought their house together four years previously, they had taken out a mortgage with the bank where he worked and now they wanted to look at a better deal.

"Cheaper, if possible," added Elle.

Mary had been on training courses where she had been taught about how to 'read' customers. She would have guessed that Gerry liked to make the decisions about finances. If he had worked in a bank then she could imagine that he had told Elle that he understood these things, with a slight hint of the patronising man to him. Elle was no wallflower, but maybe she guessed that she had less experience than him with these things? Mary livened up filling in the official forms by filling in her suspicions at the same time.

"Age?" she asked and Gerry replied, "36" and Elle replied, "33".

"Have you had a mortgage before the one you took out when you moved in together?" asked Mary.

"I did," replied Gerry as Elle shook her head, "I had one when I was ..."

His voice trailled off and Mary nodded to herself and wrote 'married' by his name on her notepad.

"Full names?"

"Gerard Sean Sawyers" and "Estelle Emma Fleming" were the answers. So, thought Mary, he has been married before but he is not married now, though he has been with her for at least four years and that is only going from when they first had property together.

"Dependents?" she asked.

"No," replied Elle.

"No, but we might be having children in the course of this mortgage deal," added Gerry.

Elle looked at her partner rather furiously at this point, Mary thought, suggesting that it was not a conversation that they had had or perhaps it was a conversation that they had had too often.

"I book hotels and other kinds of accommodation for companies and charities," said Elle, changing the subject and eyeing Mary's form for what the next question would be.

"I'm in Subsidence now," added Gerry.

"Aren't we all?" quipped Mary, but their stony faces suggested that they were not a couple for quips.

"Your drink, Madam," said the waiter, bringing it over to place on the table in front of Mary.

"Thank you," she said to the waiter before turning back to her customers to ask if they had brought any evidence of their identity and financial position.

Gerard shuffled through a set of papers and passed over copies of driving licences, utility bills and bank statements.

"Thank you," said Mary again, "I am going to take a copy of all these using my phone and then print them out for our files when I am back in the office. Meeting in a pub is not always convenient."

Gerry and Elle looked around the pub while Mary scanned the documents using her phone. Gerry noted that the waiter was hovering again. It was hardly that surprising given that they were the only people in the back room restaurant, but it was still unsettling. The guy had a hipster beard too and Gerry had never liked hipster beards.

Elle squeezed his hand and Gerry looked over at her. This was a financial journey that they were taking together and although the advisor was being a bit ridiculously thorough with the financial checks, he thought that this would mean a better mortgage deal so that they could have some more money for planning their family.

For Elle, there was something slightly romantic for her in doing anything together that built their future. It had been hard to persuade her boss to let her have some time off for this meeting, but she was glad that they had done it together. Gerard was always a little bit patronising in financial matters because of his history with the bank and she was not going to let him make what he thought would be the best decisions without her.

Mary started scanning through all the direct debits on the bank statement. Occasionally she stopped and said something like 'electricity?' or 'Council Tax?' and they would both nod. There was something oddly romantic about this, Mary thought. She was going through the financial ties that bound a couple together and although she could tell that Gerard and Estelle had a love based on practicality as well as romance, she was still glad to see it. She dealt with enough mortgages for people getting divorced and they were never quite as happy.

"Oh, what's this?" Mary asked, stopping at an unusual payment, "The King Charles Hotel?"

"That must be a mistake," said Elle, "we've never been there."

"It does happen," said Mary, "but you should really be in touch with your bank about that. Any mortgage lender will go through your financial state in small details and banks are not always the most responsible people with …"

"Banks don't make mistakes," said Gerry, feeling the need to defend his previous employers, "I am sure that we can clear it up. I'll take care of it, Elle."

Mary continued scanning through the bank statement, running a pen down along each line so that she could match the payments on the right with the payees on the left. She ticked off life insurance and car insurance and then stopped.

"Oh," she said.

"What?" asked Gerard.

"Is everything all right with your soda, Madam?" said the waiter, arriving at the table seemingly from nowhere, "are you sure we can't tempt you with the gherkins?"

"No, thank you," replied Mary and the waiter retreated behind the bar, where he pretended to polish some beer pumps.

"What were you saying?" asked Gerard.

"Well, I don't want to offend you Mr Sawyers, I know your background in banking, but ... well ... I have to tell you, there is another payment to the King Charles Hotel here."

"Let me have a look at that!"

Gerard grabbed the bank statements and scanned through them. Elle tried to look over his shoulder, but was surprised when he angled his body away from her, so she could not see what he was looking at.

"Darling?" she asked.

"It must be a mistake," he said, flicking through the papers without reading them.

"The King Charles ... what, the one in town?" asked Elle.

"It wouldn't list location, Ms Fleming, you would have to take that up with your bank. I am sure that your husband can sort it out."

Mary cursed herself as she heard these words. She had already decided that there was something slightly sexist about Gerard's wish to be in control of this couple's finances but she had not meant her words as anything more than an observation that he had said that he would be looking into it. Plus she accidentally married them. She was normally better at this than that.

"Okay," said Gerry with a sigh, "I do know why it's on there. Sometimes I like to ... just ... well, sometimes I take a break, you know? When I say that I am going away for work, I only go as far as the King Charles. It's just for a little ... peace."

Elle looked at him with both surprise and annoyance at herself for not having noticed the entry on their bank statements and for having trusted his 'work trips'.

"So, you can't get peace and quiet at home, then?" she asked.

"No, no, no, I don't mean that, I just mean sometimes I need alone time. You know?"

"No."

"Perhaps we could look at the loan to value rate? It's very much in your favour ..." said Mary trying to restore her own version of peace.

"I love you, Elle, but sometimes ... look, what about when I'm away, don't you enjoy having the house to yourself? You said that sometimes!"

Elle disliked him for saying this in such a confrontational way but also disliked him for being right. She was not going to forgive him for deceiving her, but he did have a point.

"Why couldn't you just tell me?" she asked.

"I ... I suppose that ..." he stammered and then reached out under the table and placed a hand on her leg as his own kind of awkward apology.

"If you have the funds, overpayment can be a good option," continued Mary, hoping that a deal could now be rescued from their disagreement.

Gerard placed the bank statements back on the table and sat back in his chair. He was not quite so confident now, but he nodded at Mary to go on and explain what their options were.

"If you pay more than the required rate, you are paying down the capital and that is capital you won't have to pay interest on in future ..."

"Hold on," said Estelle suddenly, her gaze having wandered to the papers on the table again, "I know the King Charles. We booked that youth workers group for their conference last week. That's the double room rate, not the single."

"I can explain ..." started Gerard with slightly too much of an edge of guilt in his voice.

"You can explain regularly going to a hotel and staying in a double room? Who is she, just tell me that?"

"She's not a she, she's a he."

"And that makes it better how?" snapped Estelle, picking up the bank statements and waving them in his face as if they were the wrong brand of lipstick discovered on his shirt.

"Maybe we ought to look at some different options ..." started Mary again.

"He's been doing that already from the sound of it!" snapped Elle.

Ah well, thought Mary, they can do quips after all. However, she was seeing this deal retreating before her eyes.

"This really is only a check to see if a mortgage provider would raise questions over your financial activities," continued Mary, no longer looking at the couple who were studiously ignoring each other's existence.

"You could have told me is all I'm saying," muttered Elle.

"I couldn't, not after ..."

"It's not Mandy, is it?"

"Amanda Fairfield? Hardly!"

"No, Amanda Buckingham. Hold on, why did you think that I meant Amanda Fairfield? It's not Amanda Fairfield, is it?"

"I told you," said Gerard, now sounding as patronising as he did when he insisted on dealing with the finances for the couple, "It's not a she. If you must know it's Stephen Ash. Steve likes getting away from things too so we have a grand booze-up and crash at the King Charles."

"Stephen with the big hands?"

"I wouldn't know."

Mary had come across these situations before, sometimes the mortgage process could bring out the worst in people and she tried to soothe the situation, even though she could see simmering resentment in both her clients.

"We ought to consider whether we want a two year or a five year product at this point," she said.

"Don't know how long he's going to be around," replied Elle.

"Oh, that's it! I'm not going to put up with this!" said Gerard angrily and stood up. He was in two minds as to whether to grab the bank statements before storming out but decided against it.

There was a silence at the table as the two women watched him walk out of the back room and wondered if anyone was going to try to call him back.

"I'm sorry," said Mary, "mortgages, houses, marriage, children, I realise, these are all the big decisions."

Gerard strode across the pub towards the front door.

The waiter was about to call out to him to ask if anything was the matter, but decided that it was not his job so long as there was someone left at the table to pay the bill and leave the tip.

Gerard stepped straight out of the pub into the path of a white van which was travelling too fast along narrow country roads. It knocked him into the wall of the pub and to the ground as it sped past.

* * * * *

Elle was holding Gerard's hand when he awoke in hospital. He had been awake before but had been incoherent and this was lost from his memory. This time he came round to the vague sensation of her hand holding his and a great deal of pain. He could see by the concern in her face how serious it was. He tried to move.

"Oww!"

"Don't move," said Elle, calmly.

"It's like ... there's just this pain in my lower back ..."

"There's a lot of swelling and we won't know until that has gone down how much of the damage is permanent."

It was only as Elle said these words and he heard the effort she was making to put as much calmness into them as possible that Gerard realised that there were areas of his body where he was struggling to feel anything. He was bandaged too.

"I'm sorry," he said and rested his head back on the hospital pillow, "I'm just really, really sorry."

"It'll be okay," said Elle, squeezing his hand, "we don't have to worry about anything else, we just need to make sure that you get better. We can make big decisions another time."

(2)

Gerry was not impressed when Mary arrived at the pub late, though she seemed to have all the right paperwork in her briefcase. He was already on edge about doing anything financial with Elle. He felt that as he had worked in a bank, he ought to know everything about financial products and that Elle would rely on him to be the expert. He felt inadequately prepared for any of this.

"I'm Gerry," he said, shaking Mary's hand, "it's okay, we ate already."

Elle shook Mary's hand as well and she explained about meeting people in pubs. It was a good idea, he wished that they had implemented it while he was at the bank, saved him from an office of four white walls and Amanda's souvenirs from southern Spain.

Truth was, he was not much of a banker. That is probably why they had made him redundant. He had never told Elle this, she thought he had just decided to leave during a restructure, but he was pretty clearly going to be axed when they started to cut back on the business banking department.

Mary seemed to know the pub and its history, which was odd for someone who Gerry estimated at around sixty. She had thick grey hair and heavy glasses and these, to him, were a sign of age.

By contrast, Elle was quite impressed with the older woman. She remembered when her school class was divided into two groups for sex education – everyone wanted to be in Mrs Hanley's class and not Miss

Polegate's class. Mrs Hanley had four children and possibly a grandchild too so she clearly knew about sex whereas Miss Polegate was a polite and petite young woman who had barely reached thirty, had no children and so clearly had no knowledge of sex. Even though in later years Elle had started to realise that perhaps her memory of Miss Polegate suggested that the teacher had some knowledge of effective contraception, she still felt more trusting of older women.

Mary certainly seemed efficient or, at least, she wrote a lot of notes on her notepad and pronounced 'Yr Hen Alarch' impeccably.

"Battered gherkins?" asked a waiter who had been hovering near the table since Mary came in.

"I beg your pardon?" asked Mary.

"Well Madam, I really meant your young friends here. Many people match a burger with our battered gherkins. They are served with a thousand island dressing and are quite a speciality in the locality ..."

Gerry looked at the waiter with some annoyance. Elle caught sight of this and placed a hand on his arm, stopping him speak.

"I'll have a soda water with a dash of lime, please," said Mary

"We have important decisions ..." started Gerry, but Elle interrupted him.

"Go on, let's have some," she said.

"Really? Battered gherkins?"

"With a thousand island dressing," added the waiter as if this would make all the difference.

Elle rubbed her partner's arm and then squeezed his hand. Gerry smiled and squeezed her hand back.

"Yes, we'll have some battered gherkins please," he said to the waiter.

"Very good, Sir."

"You should listen to me more often," teased Elle and they both laughed as if they were sharing a joke that had been told many times. While they did this, Mary was praising the decor of the pub, the narrow entrance on to the street and the comfortable surroundings.

"This is my card and the details for Garvey & Garvey," she said, "if you ever have a complaint then you can call that number. However, our aim is to get you the best mortgage possible. What is it you are looking for?"

Mary drew a star next to the name 'Gerard (male)' on her notepad. This is where her training courses would help. It was all about the story, finding out what made people tick and what made a couple want to make a large financial commitment with one another. The star indicated that Gerry clearly liked to take the lead in talking about financial things.

Mary added their ages and then the interesting detail that Gerry had been married before. She would like to have asked how long for and why it broke up, but that would have been curiosity rather than fulfilling banking regulations. She did have to ask about children. It caused more jotting on her notepad and she could see

Elle straining her neck and trying to see upside down what she had written.

Elle was happy answering all the standard questions. She was expecting all this. She assumed that they would move on to medical history, lifestyle and all the things that she had been warned by friends that she might have to talk about. They would need to talk about life insurance, critical illness cover and making a will, of course. Her mother would tell her that the two of them had to marry to 'show commitment' but you could hardly get a bigger commitment than saying that you wanted to spend most of your life in debt with someone.

"Your drink, Madam," said the waiter, bringing it over to place on the table in front of Mary.

"Thank you," she said to the waiter, thinking it was good to have attentive staff in *Yr Hen Alarch*, as she asked for her clients' evidence of identity and financial position.

Mary had two children, two sons who were now happily married with variable mortgage deals that would need to be reviewed before the next base rate change. As she scanned the documents using her work phone, she pondered that whereas her sons had stopped embracing technology once they had finished playing computer games at university, she could see her grandchildren growing up thinking that scanning things with your phone was normal. She did too now.

Mary liked the couple in front of her. She would fix a mortgage for a serial killer if she had to – that is, if he had the right documents and ability to pay– but it was always lovely to see the little gestures. Elle had squeezed her partner's hand, he had smiled back at her, he had put his hand on her leg ... it was all these little gestures that made her want to help them take on a greater debt. She could look at it as strangely romantic.

The bank statements rarely showed anything too interesting. Sometimes it was funny to see a couple panic as they realised that there was a payment to a sex toy company in between the direct debits for gas and electricity, but Mary had seen it all and never flinched. In fact, it surprised her more that people charged things to their joint account quite so freely. For some reason, a payment to a local hotel caught her attention.

"Oh, what's this? The King Charles Hotel?"

"That must be a mistake," said Elle, "we've never been there."

That was what Mary thought. She had come across scams where people steal accounts and then charge hotels and especially late night movies to other people's accounts. Knowing how to scan documents on her phone did not make her ignorant of how technology could be misused. People were too trusting in her opinion.

"I am sure that we can clear it up," Gerry was saying.

Ugh, thought Mary, he really is a model of male pride. He needs to calm down a bit and trust his partner more. Maybe his ex-wife questioned his capabilities? Who knew, but she felt a little hurt on Elle's behalf. This could be why she stopped when she saw the next payment. Perhaps she did want to burst Gerry's bubble of confidence a bit and prove to Elle that she too needed to be watching their finances.

"Oh," said Mary.

"What?" asked Gerry.

"Your battered gherkins will be a little bit longer," said the waiter, who had once again hovered over to the table, from his position behind the bar pretending to polish the beer pumps.

"What were you saying?" asked Gerry.

Mary stared at him for a moment. What was she saying before a sudden thought about why anyone would batter a gherkin? She was disliking Gerry for his male ego but, as she looked at him now, she remembered how loving these two had looked and she thought that whatever the thought had been, she could let it go. She put the last page of the bank statement down on the table while she looked for more direct debits to check.

"Hold on," said Elle, glancing over at the statement on the table, "there's another payment to the King Charles! Darling?"

"It must be a mistake," said Gerry, not looking at them.

"The King Charles ... what, the one in town?" asked Elle.

"It wouldn't list location, Ms Fleming, you would have to take that up with your bank. I am sure that your husband can sort it out," said Mary, now feeling the need to defend Gerry after telling herself off for judging his sexism.

"Okay," said Gerry with a sigh, "I do know why it's on there. Sometimes I like to ... just ... well, sometimes I take a break, you know? When I say that I am going away for work, I only go as far as the King Charles. It's just for a little ... peace."

Mary could see this situation unravelling quickly. You should be totally honest about your finances. It was part of what she and her husband had believed, along with patience, a sense of humour and always saying 'please' and 'thank you'. It had worked well enough for them that they were now looking forward to retirement together. She had to stop these two bickering somehow, she had to bring them back to the man who hooked his hand into the rip in his partner's ripped jeans and the woman who visibly warmed at his touch.

"Perhaps we could look at the loan to value rate? It's very much in your favour ..." said Mary trying to restore her own version of peace.

They were still arguing. Mary was wondering how she and Peter had ever managed to negotiate these dangerous corners.

"Why couldn't you just tell me?" Elle was asking.

"If you have the funds, overpayment can be a good option," continued Mary, "if you pay more than the required rate, you are paying down the capital and that is capital you won't have to pay interest on in future ..."

Mary had only got so far in her damage limitation exercise before she was interrupted again. To be honest, she believed Gerry. He looked like one of those men who did not tell his partner things 'to avoid upsetting her'. It was another form of sexism of course, but she thought that he looked young and stupid rather than malicious. Mind you, there were young and stupid women out there who were attracted to seeing their own faults in a man. They were still arguing. Mary felt rather awkward and tapped a few buttons on her phone. They were Morse code for SOS but no help came. It would have been a good moment for that bearded chap to come over and ask about their meal. Dammit, why had the battered gherkins not arrived already?

"She's not a she, she's a he," said Gerry as if that would calm the situation.

"Maybe we ought to look at some different options ..." started Mary again to try to stop Elle waving the bank statements in Gerry's face as some kind of paper accusation.

"He's been doing that already from the sound of it!" snapped Elle.

"This really is only a check to see if a mortgage provider would raise questions over your financial activities," continued Mary, no longer looking at the couple who were studiously ignoring each other's existence.

There is sometimes a point where you have to give up on trying to sell financial products to a couple. However, Mary was determined that this couple could return to where they were. In fact, perhaps the honesty of buying a mortgage product together would bring out the best in them.

"I told you," said Gerry, "It's not a she. If you must know it's Stephen Ash. Steve likes getting away from things too so we have a grand booze-up and crash at the King Charles."

"Stephen with the big hands?"

"I wouldn't know."

Maybe it would not bring out the best in them, thought Mary. One more attempt to focus their minds on the longer term might work.

"We ought to consider whether we want a two year or a five year product at this point," she said.

"Don't know how long he's going to be around," replied Elle.

"Oh, that's it! I'm not going to put up with this!" said Gerry angrily and stood up, eyeing the bank statements as if in thought about them.

There was a silence at the table as the two women watched him walk out of the back room and wondered if anyone was going to try to call him back.

"I'm sorry," said Mary, "mortgages ..."

"No, no, no, it's okay," said Elle, not looking as if it was okay, "it's everything. You know, marriage, children, families ... it's a tough time, a time of big decisions."

Gerard strode across the pub and he was about to throw open the front door when the waiter called over to him.

"Your battered gherkins, Sir?"

He stopped and looked at the man as if he were speaking an alien language.

"Your battered gherkins," repeated the waiter, pointing at the dish in his hand.

"I have more important decisions to make than about battered gherkins!" snapped Gerard.

While he paused to snap at the waiter, outside a white van drove past the front door quickly on its way to the next village.

The Wrong Sister

"Amanda Collins," said Mr Turlow, jumping forward with an outstretched hand for me to shake.

"No," I replied in a way that I had replied many times before.

I also knew his reaction. There would be a pause, a re-evaluation of the face in front of him (my nose is larger, my eyes slightly more set back ...) and then a realisation followed by a sudden stab of sadness.

"Oh, I'm sorry, Miss Collins, when your sister was working here ..."

"There's no need to explain," I said with forced cheeriness.

It should have been obvious to him. I was waiting for an interview, my famous sister would have walked straight in to the building and past him. All the same, Mr Turlow mumbled an awkward apology, his eyes looking anywhere but mine and then he led me towards the interview room. I wobbled on my unfamiliar heels but remained as stable as I could. These were her shoes too, grabbed from the wardrobe of her things that my parents keep at their house. The shoes pinch and these smaller footsteps I have to make in my smart clothes leave me struggling to keep up with Mr Turlow. It felt like a mile here from the train station with sore feet. I clutch my presentation under my arm and try to keep up.

Of course he knew Amanda. Everyone knew Amanda. Her career was never anything but glittering. One of the top students in school at eighteen, star of her University seminars at nineteen, a first class degree followed by a year's travelling on the money she had saved at twenty-two, fast-tracked into a graduate recruitment scheme and star of her company's advertising literature at twenty-four, returned to school to talk about how to succeed at twenty-six, dead at thirty.

* * * * *

I never saw her body. Of course, I see her face every day when I look in the mirror. I defiantly curl my eyelashes in a way that she never did and shape my eyebrows a little less cleanly that she would have done but except for the nose and perhaps the setting of the eyes, that is her face too. I had a boyfriend who never looked in the mirror other than to see his chin when he was shaving and I remember avoiding the mirror too after she died. You have to take a good look at yourself eventually though.

I never saw her body. I am not sure now if my parents wanted to spare me the trauma or whether they themselves were too traumatised to realise that I might have wanted to see her. A parent once told me that the worst thing that a child can do is die before their parents. We were supposed to be talking about me when he said that to me. Even in death, Amanda robbed people of their interest in me.

Mr Turlow shows me where I will make my presentation and I smile and nod to the interview panel, two men and a woman. I think that I can see the more elderly gentleman on the end mouth the words, "Is this the sister of the one who died?"

Amanda was a campaigner and so the newspapers still run articles about her when they can link it to a story. She is now one of those people fated to never grow old. She was thirty when she died, I am now thirty-two. My only advantage over her growing up was always being younger and in death she has stolen that from me too.

* * * * *

I know that I must sound bitter. I am not. I loved Amanda like a brother. I respected her too, though right now I wish that she had bought more comfortable shoes. My parents still cannot look in that wardrobe where they tidied away everything to do with her.

All through school I was told, 'you should be more like your sister' and I admired her too. She was charming and interesting and thoughtful and kind and clever. Her boyfriends wanted to talk to her about art and museums, my boyfriends wanted to drink cider on the golf course. I must sound jealous. Truth was, I just accepted that she had her life and I had mine - until she had no life.

Has anyone ever shined a bright light in your eyes? That was what it was like. There was a time after she died when people stopped crying and we were told endlessly that we had to 'move on'. Then it was as though this light swung round and suddenly shined on me, starkly and painfully. I was the younger Collins sister, the one who had a career of dull underachievement, suddenly expected to blaze the same trail. She had been involved in charity work, I was supposed to do that. Even her campaign for safe cycle lanes, the very thing that had killed her, was supposed to become my cause. I tense my body and clench my fists just thinking about the news reports about me which introduce me by saying, "Miss Collins, who tragically lost her own sister in a cycling accident and ..."

I never saw her body. I think that the most that my parents saw of her was her face because the injuries were so severe. Amanda managed to die with her face barely marked though. She was in the wrong place at the wrong time, but she still managed to look beautiful.

* * * * *

"Of course, we know you from your road safety campaign," says the Chair of the Panel, an enthusiastic-looking man with a slight American twang hidden in his accent.

I do wonder if this company has a 'blind' recruitment policy where people's applications have their names removed or whether they saw mine and wondered if I was related to their former star.

"Yes, well, after the ... err ... tragic circumstances ..."

I pause. This is really for the drama. It was Amanda who won the school drama prize for a 'surprisingly mature performance in A Streetcar Named Desire' according to the school newspaper. I should know the line, I wrote it. Bitter? I was writing up the triumphs of my brilliant sister.

The panel are looking at me now. I have done my presentation and they have been through an exercise with me where I had to sell them everyday objects. I suppose that I ought to start with what they want.

"Obviously I am indebted to the work that Amanda did in launching this campaign, I know that it was a passionate cause for her ... for us. Growing up we often looked on this as something we were interested in."

We had pink bicycles and Amanda's was bigger than mine and had a better saddle.

"O'Healihan-Coomelly takes its corporate social responsibility very seriously," the elder man is saying now, "and your sister was very committed to promoting the company's social benefits."

I smile at the compliment that I take on her behalf. I would like to say 'screw you all and notice me for a change'. I would like to retire to the Swansea Valley and raise alpacas or something, but there is a family duty on me to fill her place, to carry on her good work, to carry the torch or whatever other phrase the local paper is going to use this week. Instead, I am going to get a job in PR, the very same PR firm where she worked. I know that I am not fully qualified for this but I also know that my name means a lot to them.

I answer some more questions and then the Chair of the Panel says what he has been dying to say all interview.

"It must be hard for you to fill her shoes."

"It's painful," I say, answering truthfully on several counts.

* * * * *

I got the job. Yay me or rather Yay Amanda, looking out for her little sis to the end, laying the path that I will then walk down. Maybe I will go to Swansea and raise alpacas. It does not have to be alpacas, it could be llamas, I am not fussy. I just want to do something that is different to what she did. I know that my parents will love me doing this job like big sis though and it is the sensible thing to do. I always was the sensible one.

I am happy with the job and do it in a dull and unspectacular way that disappoints some of the people who have been there longer than four years. I am fine with it, but I can tell what they are thinking. They are thinking that the wrong sister died. That is not the problem. The problem is that I agree.

God's Filing Card System

"*Eu chamo-me Colin,*" said Colin shakily - 'I am called Colin', "*Eu sou da Inglaterra.*" – 'I am from England.'

Colin's tutor Luis squinted as if this would help him listen to Colin's accent better.

"Mmm ...," he said with an accent that was only five years Cardiff but twenty-five years Oporto, "you sound a bit French. Not '*Angleterre*' remember, in Portuguese you come from '*Inglaterra*', pronounce the 'i'."

"*Obrigado*," said Colin with a little more certainty, 'thank you' he could manage.

Luis moved around the classroom to listen to some of the other learners. Colin envied them. Sophie at the end, she was Scottish and learning Portuguese to impress a new boyfriend, there was Debra who was going travelling for three months in Brazil, Liz and Steve a retired couple who were just doing it for fun and then on the other side of him Samantha who loved languages and wanted to learn more and Harmony who ... actually, he had no idea what Harmony was doing in the class, but this was not the point. Colin was the only one taking a class in 'Portuguese for Beginners' because his workplace had told him to do it. We are opening an office in Lisbon they said, go and learn how to say please and thank you to them and you can be our link person. Great, now he lost every Thursday night to coping with the idea that there were plural forms of colours.

Steve turned to him and said hello or rather '*ola*'. Steve was an amiable man, clearly using his retirement to try the 'mad scientist' look of wild, white hair and slightly mismatched clothes. He had great enthusiasm for the subject though and sitting next to him meant practice in every spare moment of the lesson.

"*Eu sou de Hereford,*" said Steve – 'I am from Hereford', "*E você?*" - 'And you?'

"*Eu sou de Cardiff,*" replied Colin – 'I am from Cardiff' although actually he was from a small town near to the border with England where his mother had moved a couple of years after he was born. He had moved about four or five times during his childhood, sometimes over in to England, sometimes back to Wales and it had left him never quite sure whether he should claim a link to *Inglaterra* or to *País de Gales*.

Colin reached for his flask of coffee and carefully poured himself out a drink. Evening classes were not all bad, he supposed, he just wished that when they talked about the basic information he had something more exciting to talk about. He wished that he could lie about his life.

* * * * *

The wind swirled the brown leaves around Colin's feet as he walked along the road towards his place in the terrace. The wind was becoming colder with each day and he held his coat tightly around his chest, thinking of the approaching winter.

He placed one hand on the door while the other reached into his pocket to find his house keys. The door was always hard to get through but after a little of the daily fiddling with the key it swung open for him. He stepped inside his house and was immediately reminded that he needed to turn up the heating. He stumbled through the dark of the front room and turned on the light. Home sweet home, he thought.

Colin took off his coat and arranged it on the correct hanger in the hall and then went upstairs to place his bag in the correct place in his bedroom.

Back in the kitchen, he looked at the whisky bottle and poured himself a small measure before wondering what to do with the second half of the evening. When you were at school you had homework, when you were a teenager you had nights out and when you were first in a job you had 'work dos' (and work don'ts). Friends who had married and had children would now spend their time amusing their kids but what you do in your mid thirties if you are single and living alone?

Colin drank his whisky in one gulp. What he needed was a hobby, he muttered to himself, maybe he should join an evening class.

* * * * *

"Tonight," announced Luis, "we will be looking at *familia*. That is the family. So, how do we talk about family?"

Colin took out his notebook and started to write down the words that were being written on the board at the front of the class. These would be useful for if he made small talk with business contacts, he decided. The only problem was that most of them were irrelevant to him - his parents were only children so there were no aunts and no uncles. His grandparents had died when he was a child, a teenager and a young adult respectively. There was no *esposa* - no wife - to talk about and so no in-laws and no children - no *filhos* - to talk about. Colin looked again as Luis rubbed '*esposa*' off the board and said that there was a different word for wife though it would depend on whether you were learning European or Brazilian Portuguese. Colin dutifully wrote down the European word. However, he could not help but feel slightly annoyed at the lack of cousins and other relatives in his life to give him some practice. Being an only child had been fun in many ways but he had always secretly hoped to find a band of close friends to be his 'gang' or at least drinking buddies who went to the same pub every Friday after work to review the week's events. Yet somehow he had always ended up on his own.

"Now, you turn to your partner and tell them about your *familia*," Luis said somewhat predictably.

Liz was saying '*Olá*' to him and starting to talk about her grandchildren. Colin smiled and nodded as if he were interested, this was a simulation after all. A simulation, he thought? Then why should any of it be true?

"*Eu tenho três irmãs*," he found himself saying - 'I have three sisters', "*Elas chamo-se Sarah, Lucy e Hannah.*"

Liz nodded and was about to ask about them when Luis interrupted.

"I think we shall take a break there, take ten minutes and then we come back to us," he said.

Colin reached for his flask of coffee, prepared specially in advance of course, and was surprised that Liz kept speaking to him.

"Three sisters? That must have been tough growing up - older or younger?"

"Oh, all older," said Colin, without thinking about it, "Sarah was the oldest by some way. She's married with two grown up children at university. Time has gone by so quickly with them. She works part-time in the university library."

"Three sisters did you say?" said Liz's husband Steve, listening in and leaning over, "I always wanted a sister but I had a brother."

"Lucy is the go-getter - she works all hours with a fancy law firm in the centre of Cardiff. Used to be married but divorced now, shame for the kids, isn't it?" continued Colin, warming to his imaginary life.

"I'll bet that Hannah was the baby of the group then," added Liz.

Colin took a slurp of coffee as he thought about his imaginary family.

"Well, as much of a baby as someone can still be in their mid or late thirties. She's still a really attractive woman mind you, there's not a man who doesn't fancy her to this day."

Steve nodded and drank from a bottle of water.

"Oh love, would you go and get me something chocolatey from the machine?" asked Liz of her husband.

"Ah, sure," he replied, not really wanting to leave the conversation but knowing that he was going to have to go.

Liz smiled at Colin who nodded sympathetically though not really knowing why.

After the break, Luis decided to move on to a review of the previous week's homework and so there was no more talk of the fictitious family. That is, there was no more talk of it until Colin was walking out of the Modern Languages building and Steve asked him if he was close to his family.

"Oh yeah," replied Colin, "we see each other every week - especially after our parents ... well, you know ..."

Steve nodded as he headed towards his car.

"I lost touch with most of my relatives, you're a lucky man. Anyway, see you *próxima semana*."

Colin looked blank and shrugged.

"Oh sorry, we haven't done that yet, have we? 'Next week'."

"We're doing it next week?"

"No, 'next week'."

"Yes, next week."

They stared at each other and Steve decided that he would simply go and get the car to pick up Liz rather than trying to explain further.

* * * * *

The wind swirled the brown leaves around Colin's feet as he walked along the road towards his place in the terrace. The wind was becoming colder with each day and he held his coat tightly around his chest, thinking of the approaching winter.

He placed one hand on the door while the other reached into his pocket to find his house keys. This time the door swung open and he heard music and saw light inside. Standing in front of him was a woman who looked familiar. She had greying, curly hair that hung to her shoulders and she was older than him, but she also looked a little bit like him. For some reason he was not scared to see a stranger in his house, but smiled instead. The woman looked at him with a shrug as if to say 'why aren't you coming in?'

Now a younger woman walked down the stairs. She was more like Colin's age but dressed very differently. The older woman was all loose fitting clothes and comfort, but this woman wore a tight top, a leather skirt that reached her knees and dark boots. Unlike the first stranger, she was heavily made up and her black hair was scraped back behind her head.

"Hey bruv," she said, touching his arm and tugging on his coat to pull him into the house, "you've taken your time tonight!"

When he felt her touch, Colin experienced a strange kind of bolt of electricity through him. It was only a momentary contact but it brought him inside and made him feel ... hold on, he thought, I may have only just met her, but there is no way that I am attracted to my sister!

How did he know that that was his sister? Why was he not more upset to find women in his house? He looked into the front room as the younger woman walked in there and then raised his eyes to her head level. He needed space to think.

"I'm just going upstairs to put my things down," he said.

"Don't be long, I'm serving up!" came a shout from the kitchen.

He wanted to shout back sarcastically 'of course, Mum!' but stopped himself, partly because he had no idea why he would say that.

Colin climbed the stairs wearily, pausing only to hang his coat on a hook next to the coat for Spring, the coat for Summer, the coat for Autumn and the fake fur coat that Hannah always wore when she visited. Colin shook his head and carried on walking. He needed to make sense of this.

Upstairs in his house, Colin was relieved to find that the usual layout of two bedrooms and a bathroom had not changed. He left the bag containing his Portuguese homework by his bedside table. It would stay there until he had completed the homework for that week. He had a system and he disliked his system being disturbed.

His work shoes were taken off and went under the bed and he sighed as he removed his tie. Colin decided that he just needed to calm down, take a long shot of whisky and relax in front of a mindless soap opera or a tedious drama on television. He would be okay.

He made his way out of the bedroom along the upstairs landing to the bathroom. He was starting to like the sound of his plan, especially the part with the whisky. He reached for the bathroom door handle and found that it did not move when he pulled it. Bloody hell, he thought, was it broken again? When was he going to be allowed time off to oversee someone fixing that? He tugged on it again to see what would happen.

"Do you mind? Give me a minute!" shouted a voice from inside. It was a female voice.

"Sorry, sis!" he said reflexively. What the hell did that mean?

The door opened after a minute and Colin's confused face was greeted by the sight of a third woman, not as old as the first woman but definitely older than him and Hannah and dressed as though she had been sitting at an important desk all day.

"Little bruv!" she said and smiled at his dislike of the phrase, "I didn't realise you were back. Good, we can eat. Mum has been cooking up a storm down there."

Colin wanted to smile at the thought that his mother was alive and still cooking for him but there was something about the way that Lucy – oh hold on, this was Lucy then? – said the word 'Mum' that loaded it with sarcasm.

"Sarah, you mean?" he said timidly.

Lucy leaned forward and made a gentle knocking on the side of his head, "Has Portuguese knocked the sense out of you? Of course Sarah, who the hell else would we call 'Mum'?"

With that, Lucy walked downstairs. Colin stared at her for a moment and smiled weakly, but Lucy was muttering to herself something about always knowing that her little brother was weird. He guessed that he was intended to hear it.

Colin decided not to follow his usual ritual and partially undress for dinner. It was a single man in his thirties thing to do he knew, but he thought that there was a certain pleasure to cooking in your own home in your underwear. The freedom to do what he wanted in his own house was one of the few privileges of his life, but he would give it a miss this time. There was another shout from downstairs and Colin hurriedly went down to the kitchen.

It was hard to fit four adults around the dining table at the end of the kitchen but somehow they managed it as if this was something that they did every Thursday night.

"Thank you for joining us, little bruv," said Lucy with sarcasm and they all chose their usual places to sit while Sarah served her complicated casserole and rice creation.

"Now, now," said Sarah waving a food-covered stirring spoon over a full, large saucepan, "you should just remember that I had it easy for ten years before you lot came along. I could have done being an only child and then you lot spoiled it for me!"

There was laughter, but laughter that recognised that this had been said many times before.

"Where are the kids tonight?" asked Hannah as they all ate.

"The Sperm Donor's got them," replied Lucy, causing raised eyebrows, which Colin realised were not at his long-established title, but at his sudden interest in fatherhood, "I don't expect it to be more than a phase, but while he wants to play Dad, he can do it."

"Still can't believe that he ..." Hannah started to mutter, but her voice trailled off as if she knew that everyone else would be in agreement with whatever she was going to say.

"I may get called to court tomorrow, so I need the bathroom in the morning," stated Lucy plainly, "so the likes of you who need a full face of make-up just to go to the gym need to be out of there."

The comment was clearly directed at Hannah. Colin smiled at the idea that they could all communicate without having to name who they were talking to, the comments were so well-understood.

"Well, my children are home for half term from university and are helping their father at Scouts," said Sarah without looking at anyone.

Colin felt something and was almost exhilarated by the recognition. Of course, Sarah was still married and she had just that little bit of disrespect for her divorced sister. She would never say it but then she would never need to say it. He smiled at how his family communicated with each other.

"What are you smiling at?" asked Lucy when she noticed this.

"Nothing," said Colin blankly.

"You leave our baby brother alone!" replied Hannah, giving him a mocking protective hug. Colin remembered how much he hated being called 'baby brother' but knew that this was always his name.

After dinner he offered to wash up and this was accepted. Sarah would not do it because she had cooked ('though why you cannot just buy a dishwasher I have no idea'), Lucy wanted to call The Sperm Donor to make sure that he was looking after the children okay and Hannah had only just applied a new coat of nail varnish and felt that the soapy suds would damage it.

As he was washing the dishes and listening to the rest of his family chat in the front room next door, Colin started to wonder about why they were there. I mean, he had enjoyed them visiting, but none of them seemed to want to leave. Lucy and Hannah had both been drinking and Sarah showed no sign of going. In fact, had he not heard Lucy talk about her children staying over with their father? This brought up an interesting question. When the washing up was done, he walked into the front room and asked it.

"Where are you all intending to sleep?" he asked his sisters.

Sarah looked at the others and spoke with an authority that clearly came with being the eldest.

"I will take your spare bed and Lucy can sleep on the floor in the spare room with me," she said.

"That's not fair!" protested Lucy, "Besides, I told you, I may have to be in court tomorrow, I need to be properly rested."

"You know how it goes, you can have the bed when you are older than me," replied Sarah.

"Since the age of five ..." started Lucy.

"Have you always been mother?" asked Colin, not meaning it sarcastically but realising as he said it that the rest of the family took it that way.

Sarah gave a shake of her long, greying curls.

"I am not that much older than you really," she tried to argue.

"Only one of us has a Saga Catalogue, that's all I'm saying ..." muttered Lucy.

"Me and Col will bunk up together like the old days," announced Hannah and everyone nodded except Colin.

"No, no, don't worry about that," he quickly replied, "I can sleep on the sofa in here."

"The sofa? Don't be daft, you won't fit on it!" replied Hannah.

"I don't want to be stumbling over you and smelling your unwashed socks when I am getting ready in the morning," added Lucy.

Colin sighed. He did not like the sound of this arrangement at all. Was this what families did? Was this what his family did more to the point? He had established that Hannah was an attractive woman and now she wanted to share his bed? Somehow he felt uncomfortable with this arrangement. He poured himself a whisky as a distraction.

Colin could not remember so much noise in his front room. He did once have a work-related mixer which was reasonably well-attended by colleagues, but even that was quite restrained compared to the voices cutting over one another and telling overlapping stories. It was funny, in the workplace storytelling seemed so regimented, you waited your turn, but in the family everyone could talk at once and bounce ideas off one another.

Lucy punctuated her stories with calls to The Sperm Donor to ensure that he was looking after their children. Clearly she did not trust him. She was also the queen of the cutting remark if any of them was getting a little too proud of their achievements. Sarah talked calmly about life as a part-time worker and filling the rest of her days with other activities. Meanwhile, everyone wanted to know how Hannah was doing running her gymnastics team. Colin thought that secretly they wanted to ask her if she was becoming too old for it, but she seemed to have an undimmed energy for everything from gymnastics to conversation.

Sarah was the first to say that she needed to go to bed. She had been talking less for a while and Hannah's story about the ancient rivalry between gymnastics and hockey had fizzled out and left a comfortable late evening silence.

"It's always good to meet up," said Sarah, "but you know that I can't stay out late on a week night."

"If you're going to bed, then I need to as well. I don't want you stepping over me in the night. I might need to be in court tomorrow and I need my beauty sleep," added Lucy.

The other two sisters looked at each other on the words 'beauty sleep' and Lucy simply rolled her eyes when she noticed. Some jokes did not even have to be voiced.

Colin made his own way upstairs to his bedroom and changed while Hannah worked at removing her make-up. He had managed to wash and be ready for bed in a quick time and so he lay there for a while, pondering the noise and activity of the night. He felt quite exhausted by it all. It was good, but it was exhausting. Then in walked Hannah.

Some women can simply wear cute pyjamas well, he decided as he looked at her dressed in figure-hugging pyjamas featuring characters from the Wallace and Gromit films. It helped that she had her long, black hair hanging down to her shoulders and, oddly, now that she was no longer made up she had a natural beauty that he rather liked. They did look quite similar in a way that thirty-five years of different life experience had only changed a small amount. Of course, he could tell from the line of her pyjamas that she was a lot fitter than he was. Hannah yawned and climbed into bed next to her brother without even seeming to think about it.

"Have we done a lot of this?" he asked her.

"What's wrong with you?" came the reply as she stretched a hand over and felt his brow, "Has Spanish wiped your memory?"

Colin switched out the light and Hannah cuddled up next to him in the dark. Feeling her body push against his, he instinctively shifted to one side away from it. Perhaps she thought that he had misinterpreted her action as meaning that she did not have enough room and so she moved up next to him again. This time he felt the warmth and started to enjoy it. Not in a sexual way but also not in a friendly way. Somehow there was a familiar intimacy to it that reminded him of safety and being young and scared together. He felt protective towards her. Actually, he realised that he felt protective towards all of his family - hell, if he ever got hold of The Sperm Donor, he would be in trouble for what he had done to Lucy! What had he done? Colin's head started to hurt.

"Not Spanish but .. no, did we always do this? It's just ... I'm not sure every family does this. Tell you what, humour me, explain it."

Hannah sighed and started to speak as if she was describing knowledge that he should really know.

"You remember Mam's stories? How she moved away from their father and then the two of us came along. In the early years how we all shared one room, me and you in a bed together while Mam went out and worked all hours to put food on the table? You must remember how she said we were treated? Disowned by their family, always seen as the 'illegitimates', the children who shouldn't have existed?"

Their family, thought Colin, those two women in the next room had a different father and therefore a different family.

"They really called us 'the illegitimates'? What decade did they think it was?" he asked indignantly and genuinely hurt at how they had been treated.

There was a slight pause for thought in the darkness. Hannah was weighing up how to phrase something and Colin could feel that she was stressed thinking about it.

"Because Mam left their Dad ..." she started but her voice trailled off.

"We're one happy family now though, right?" asked Colin, trying to take the stress out of the situation.

Hannah laughed and it was a laugh that floated out into the bedroom air for a few seconds before dispersing.

"Of course. That's why we argue so much."

As he lay together with Hannah in the dark, Colin thought about how he knew a pen picture of each of his family now. Maybe this, he thought, was how God did it. Somewhere in heaven there was just a vast library and God could call on Saint Peter to look up a reference in the infinite book of souls.

For instance, here was an entry on Sarah. She had had ten years of being centre stage as an only child and then suddenly along came a challenger. She had resented Lucy's destruction of her quiet home, of course, but she had soon found out that she was the mature one who everyone could look up to. Unfortunately, she grew up in a world that worshipped youth and soon she was the untrendy, out-of-touch old one in the family. Her only response was to mother them and become essential. That and bite back her annoyance of being called 'mother'.

Then there was Lucy. Lucy committed the crime of destroying Sarah's starring role in the family drama but she did more than that. A year after she was born, their mother left them with their father to start a new relationship. What would an eleven year old think of this but that the little, crying ball of puke that everyone else worshipped had destroyed her family too. Lucy grew up resented. Though things were patched over now, had she become a successful adult to try to escape the guilt of the crimes that she had committed at birth?

Of course the bond with Hannah was going to be strongest, thought Colin. They were bonded over being the 'other family', the illegitimates who were looked down on for so many years. God had painted Hannah beautiful and even in her late thirties she could do it and she knew it. She was the kid sister and yet he was the kid brother too, the one they mocked as 'little bruv' but were also protective about. Is that how he became someone with a normal job, someone with a house, someone who was trusted to learn Portuguese? He started to wonder if he was a success after all.

"Oy! Are you snoring?" asked Hannah, jabbing him in the side.

"I don't snore!" he protested, "It's you who snore!"

"Me?" came the voice through the dark, "I don't snore, it's just that sometimes I dream that I am a tractor."

There was a silence for a while until Hannah spoke again.

"Come on bruv, let's get some sleep or mother will be in to tell us off!"

Hannah rolled over away from her brother and Colin lay there in the dark for a few moments. Then they both heard Sarah coughing loudly next door and they giggled quietly to each other as if once again they were the rebellious siblings.

The next morning Colin discovered the difference that was made to your mornings by having other people in your house. He was used to falling out of bed, throwing some clothes on and grabbing some food before rushing out to work. This was not possible on that Wednesday morning. Sarah was awake first to be fair, though she made a lot of noise in the kitchen searching for pots and pans and things to cook, probably already knowing that no-one was going to have time to eat them. Lucy spent a long time in the bathroom according to Hannah who was banging on the door several times to complain that she too had a job to go to. At one point Lucy emerged from the bathroom and Hannah went and barricaded herself in, refusing to listen when Lucy returned to ask for her make-up bag from the window sill. When Colin did approach the door, Sarah came up the stairs to say that she too needed to get ready but it was okay because he could go in there with her if he did not object. Colin decided that he did object.

It was chaos and Colin decided that he did not like chaos. He liked the idea of chaos, the wild shouting and rushing around which would eventually propel all four of them out of the door on time and reasonably well-presented, but he did not like the experience of it. When they were all ready to go, he hugged each sister individually and carefully. Sarah hugged back warmly, Lucy barely kept contact as she checked her watch behind his back and Hannah was enveloping him in a big hug before he had time to approach her. He did love his family, but …

* * * * *

Colin sat down in his Portuguese class next to Liz. She had been showing pictures of her grandchildren on her phone again. Colin could not remember now what age they were or where they were on holiday, but he smiled and made appreciative noises loyally.

"It must be nice having a big family," he said to make conversation.

"What do you mean?" replied Liz, a confused look stretched across her face, "I thought you had three sisters?"

Colin laughed.

"No, you must be mistaken," he replied.

* * * * *

The wind swirled the brown leaves around Colin's feet as he walked along the road towards his place in the terrace. The wind was becoming colder with each day and he held his coat tightly around his chest, thinking of the approaching winter.

He placed one hand on the door while the other reached into his pocket to find his house keys. He unlocked the door and went in.

Inside the house was silence. He had re-learnt why he liked it.

'Peter? Would you get me the file on Colin, please,' God would say.

The file would start with 'Colin likes living on his own.'

He would miss them, but not that much.

Vegan Cheese

The first thing that you need to know about me is that I am a vegan. I never got that joke - you know, "How do you tell a vegan? Answer - There is no need, they will tell you". What is so funny about that? I am a vegan. I do not harm any non-human animals and I campaign to stop other people doing so. I deplore all forms of violence. My name is Joe, by the way.

I live with my girlfriend Sophie (also, a vegan, of course) and we are both gaming nuts. I have this great game on my phone at the moment. It is one of those clash of civilisation games and I am playing as the Austro-Hungarian Empire of the 19th century.

Austro-Hungary! It's the challenging one, you are surrounded on all sides but for me, it does not matter as I am cheating a little. If something goes well, I click on 'save'. Then I keep playing and if things do not go well, I simply quit, click on reload and there I am back at the last save point and able to play things better. I am going to crush those Germans ... well, Prussians they were back then, it is kind of a release I reckon.

It was the last Saturday in June and I was standing outside Tesco Express at the bottom of St Mary's Street in Cardiff with a shopping list in my hand. I had a simple itinerary - into the shopping centre for a card for my mother's birthday, some toothpaste in the chemist, round to the Post Office and then to a shop called 'Beanfreaks' to pick up some vegan mozzarella cheese for the dinner that Sophie was making that night.

I could hear the sound of music at the other end of the street and I could tell that the Saturday crowds were busier than normal. The atmosphere was stifling as people pushed past me and I heard someone say that it was something called 'Armed Forces Day'. Oh typical, I thought, people traipsing off to watch some celebration of violence.

I had been playing my game on my phone but the Serbs were causing trouble again, so I decided to quit and then save it. Conquest of the Balkans could wait for another day. I pushed a child out of the way to get into the shopping centre and out of the sunshine.

Beanfreaks is a great shop. Slap bang in the middle of Cardiff and all the food you could want that does not contain non-human animal products. The cheese - non-dairy, of course - is great and the guy who runs it, Stu or 'Meat-Free Stu' as he is known, always has the latest food and drink.

I had soon been through my shopping list and Beanfreaks was in sight. I could hear the sound of some kind of parade in the distance. People were moving closer and hurrying towards it, somewhere around the corner of the top of the street. I ignored them and pushed past people and into Beanfreaks.

Meat-free Stu was over by the fridge talking to Brianna. Brianna and I used to run in the same circles but we fell out. She was dressed in black and looked overheated for a warm June's day. Stu was apologising for not having made up an order for her in advance.

In Brianna's hand, grasped by her black painted fingernails, was a block of dairy-free mozzarella cheese. However, I realised with horror as I moved towards the cabinet that it was not just any block of cheese, it was the last block of dairy-free mozzarella cheese in the shop. I looked back to Stu and he shrugged apologetically.

"Hi Brianna, I need that cheese," I said reasonably.

"Sorry Joe, out of luck, I got to it first."

"But it's the last packet, Sophie needs it for tonight's meal."

"Tough, she can use cheddar or something."

"I need that cheese!" I said and made a grab for it.

Brianna was quick and pulled it out of my way. I tried to move around her but she had hidden it behind her back. She was smiling victoriously.

"You need to learn to live and let live. That was always you, wasn't it? Out protesting, out hassling people, always telling people that they were wrong."

"But when they are, they are. There's a holocaust of animals going on out there and we have to stop it!"

"There you go - a holocaust, rather anti-Semitic, don't you think? No-one changes their mind because you shout at them. No-one ever changed their mind about anything - vegan or anything else - because a stranger on the internet shouted at them. I will happily talk about it if people ask, but I would rather that they see what I do and ask about it."

"Yes and you slip quietly off into the background while animals die and ..."

At the next second, the debate was broken. There was a far off sound, a boom and a shattering of shop windows. Then there was a hush and a puzzlement and the crowds started to run back down St Mary's Street, shrieking and shouting. Stu had run out of the shop to see what had happened and Brianna followed him, taking the cheese with her. I stood there, stunned. I reached for the familiarity of my phone as the only way to cope. I needed to invade Serbia. I clicked on reload.

It was the last Saturday in June and I was standing outside Tesco Express at the bottom of St Mary's Street in Cardiff with a shopping list in my hand. The noise, the people, the sun, the whispered conversations about the parade, they were all familiar. I looked at my phone in disbelief and realised what had happened. I had clicked on save when I had already quit the game. It was everything else that had been saved! I had not returned to the last saved point in the game, I had returned to the last saved point in my life! This was incredible and I realised what this meant - that dairy-free mozzarella could be mine!

I had gone wrong before by trying to shop on my way to Beanfreaks. The street was crowded but I was sure that if I pushed through the crowd, I could make it to the store before Brianna did. A small child ran into my legs and I almost tripped over, a group of teenage girls stopped in front of me with an excited shriek, the music was growing louder from the end of the street but I was only progressing slowly.

I pushed one of the children over and he started to cry. I did try to apologise but before I could move very far, his mother had grabbed the back of my hoodie. She was remonstrating with me and telling me off about violence. I wanted to tell her that if she disliked violence then she should avoid Armed Forces Day but I had the thought of cheese pushing me on.

The heat was stifling and the crowds packed the street from side to side. The restaurants hardly helped by putting chairs and tables out in the pedestrianised street. Finally, after some pushing and shoving, I could see Beanfreaks.

I nearly screamed when I saw Meat-Free Stu walking from the counter towards the fridge.

"Sorry Bri, I meant to put your order together this morning."

"That's all right Stu," she was replying.

I saw his hand reach into the fridge and I screamed. The two of them stared at me. I mouthed the words 'I need that cheese' and they simply stood there, puzzled. I know that it must have been minutes that we stood there staring because my shock was only interrupted by a sound from around the top of the street. A shattering of shop windows followed, before a hush and a ... I clicked reload at this point.

It was the last Saturday in June and I was standing outside Tesco Express at the bottom of St Mary's Street in Cardiff with a shopping list in my hand. How did Brianna do it? If there were crowds all around for the parade, how did she make it to the shop before I did? Maybe if I had a chance to reason with her, maybe I could persuade her to give me the cheese. I would explain that this was the only vegan cheese establishment open that day and that this was an essential ingredient for Sophie's meal. She would understand. However, I had to stop the thing that interrupted us each time.

At the top of St Mary's Street is a long stretch of road in front of the castle. Looking around, it seemed pretty clear that the explosion must have come from somewhere in the area to the right. That seemed to be where people were running from the first time it happened and it made sense that you would create maximum impact if you attacked the parade as it turned the corner by the castle. It must be the bin on the corner opposite Burger King. Surely they would have checked that ... unless it was an insider or they had planted the device as the crowds converged in the area?

I pushed my way through the crowds to an unmarked white van by Burger King. They were so easy to spot, but that would work in my favour. I knocked on the window. A driver eyed me suspiciously. There was no time to make any pretence.

"There's a bomb in that bin over there," I announced, "it's going to go off in about five minutes. You need to stop the parade and clear the area."

A man in a faded baseball cap with last night's stubble still sitting on his chin stared out at me.

"We're here to mend the phones, butt," he said in a broad Valleys accent.

"Don't believe me, I know that you have heat sensitive equipment or x-rays or something. Check that bin - but I need to get out of here before it explodes."

There was a tone of panic creeping into my voice that must have made him sit up and take notice. He eyed me suspiciously, but I had no time to explain further. If they wanted to risk people's lives then they could, I would simply walk away and remain safe to ... woah, my feet almost left the ground as an arm grabbed my hoodie and hauled me off through the crowd.

He was a tall man, though I guessed at a bullet proof vest or body armour giving him some added bulk. He had a walkie talkie to his ear and he was not letting go of me, however much I mumbled 'cheese!' at him. He listened to the response on his walkie talkie and then pulled me over to a police car parked six feet further away from the corner.

"You need to start talking and you need to start talking now. X-rays have found a device in that bin and we are clearing the area. You need to explain how you knew that."

His voice was calm but angry. I could hear the sound of a crowd being told to move quickly. Fair play to them, they had managed to claim that it was a last minute route change and to close off the road quickly. They might yet manage to ...

"Well?"

I realised that this was going to be very difficult to explain. Why could they not just be happy that they had averted a disaster? I hardly had time to think of a reason before I was dragged to the car and pushed into the back seat. My phone went flying out of my trouser pocket and landed on the floor.

"We'll take that," said the man.

"No," I replied, "no, you can't."

"Maybe you should start talking quickly about who your friends are who have planned this. What is it, then? Cold feet? Realised that it's not the life for you? Start talking and we might go easy on what happens to you."

"Okay," I said, calmly, "I tell you everything I know. Can I call my girlfriend? She worries and she's making a great meal tonight and ..."

"I don't give a damn if she is spit-roasting a whole hog for you tonight, you're going to bloody talk and ..."

The tall man's words were interrupted by an explosion. This time the police car windows shattered and I could hear shrieks of people, possibly unlucky ones hit by debris. There was a kind of hush and in the deafened confusion, I leaned over and picked up my phone where it had fallen from the tall man's hand. Still no bloody cheese. I hit reload.

It was the last Saturday in June and I was standing outside Tesco Express at the bottom of St Mary's Street in Cardiff with a shopping list in my hand. What could I do? Brianna would beat me to the shop, even if I hurried. We would argue and even if I was reasonable, she would not give up the cheese. I could phone Stu but if he was already expecting her and had a shopping list prepared, I might be too late. There had to be a way. Surely I had not saved at a point that was too late in time? I had not kept a save point from an earlier position. There had to be a way.

As I pushed my way down St Mary's Street, elbowing my way past a group of teenage girls who shouted abuse after me, it struck me that I had been looking at this as the need to get to the shop before Brianna rather than looking at how I could delay Brianna from reaching the shop. I knew from our political engagements that she lived in Riverside. She had a flat in an old pub there and so she would be walking in from the west. It would be along Wellington Street, over the bridge on to Castle Street and round into Beanfreaks. She would be close even now, but I could stop her. I smiled. This was my best move since a pre-emptive strike across northern Italy prevented French expansion.

I stood in the phone box and dialled 999. I thought about accents to try - they would be recording this call of course and I did add a slight west Wales lilt to my voice. I asked for the police. Then I started in earnest -

"This is a bomb warning. You have ten minutes. There is a bomb in the golden postbox outside the newsagent to the west of the turning for St Mary's Street. This will detonate when the parade marches past. This is being done for the safety of all innocent men killed by your armed forces across the world. They must learn that they are not safe. You have ten minutes to clear the area. The code word is swordfish."

I hung up and wondered if that last touch was too much. I avoided ranting about atrocities in the Middle East or something like that as I thought that it was more genuine as a straightforward warning. I walked up the street more slowly now.

My calculation was simple. If they thought that a bomb was in the postbox, then they would clear people away from it. Brianna would be caught in the crowd being pushed over the bridge back in to Riverside by the police. Further down the road, they would push the crowd back towards Burger King leaving a gap in the middle around the postbox. Even if Brianna worked out that she could walk down Westgate Street, it would be too late. Besides, my guess would be that she would hang around in the crowd to see what was going on.

I had only travelled a few minutes up the road before I sensed that my plan was working. There was a slightly panicked hubbub up ahead and I could hear police loudhailers and sirens. It was working. The crowd was backing up, but I pushed through them until I was outside Beanfreaks.

"What's going on out there?" asked Meat-Free Stu as I entered his empty - hallelujah - shop.

"Oh, it's some kind of thing for the armed forces. You know I'm a pacifist."

"I know, aren't we all, but the crowd isn't moving. The police are kind of pushing them back down the street."

"I'd stand away from the window is all I'm saying."

There on the shelf in front of me was the last packet of dairy-free mozzarella cheese in the shop. You could not believe the width of the smile on my face. I had gone through so much for this.

"Joe!" called out Stu, "I was meant to make up a shopping bag for Brianna, I think that she wanted that. It's the last one, I'm afraid."

"She's not having it."

"Joe ..."

"I have been through so much for this cheese, I am not giving it up now!"

Stu walked towards me in what was his best threatening manner. He was only a slight man and it was hardly intimidating. He stopped and scratched his head. He was unsure of what to do or say. I think that he was calculating that he would not sell me the cheese or that perhaps he could persuade me to buy something else.

"Brianna will be here soon, you guys could talk it out then," he offered.

However, he would never know if his offer was taken. There was a sudden loud boom, a shattering of shop windows followed by a hush and then screaming more intense than before. Stu ran out to see what was going on and was nearly pushed straight back in by the crowd running away down St Mary's Street.

I pushed past him and out of the shop with the cheese. There were more of them than before. It seemed as though there had been a greater crowd around the bin and Burger King this time and so casualties were more severe. I fitted into the crowd's flow and looked behind me to see if Stu had followed. I had, after all, just performed an act of theft. He was trying to help someone collapsed near the shop though and was unconcerned about me.

The screaming crowd took me back down to Tesco Express. Up close, they were not pretty. They were running in all sorts of directions, I saw some people with blood on their faces, others clasping children closely to their chests and everywhere a look of bewilderment and shock. I suppose that I had seen it all before but no-one noticed the calm man among them.

The crowd spewed out into the road at the end of St Mary's Street. I ducked down into Caroline Street, took a right at the end and found myself between the library and John Lewis. This little bit of pedestrianised city centre was much quieter and I could sit and catch my breath.

I had done something truly amazing today and I could be proud of myself. I had taken a problem and, having been given an original way of solving it, found a solution. I tucked the cheese into my pocket. The sun was shining, it was going to be a good day.

I looked at the shopping list again. The second item was 350g of organic coconut flour. The only place I could get that was Beanfreaks. Damn ... I took out my phone and reached for the reload button.

The Tale of Charlotte the Liberator

[Note to the reader : those of you who have read the novella, 'The Tale of Charlotte the Liberator' may be surprised to discover that she started life as a short story ... the short story that follows, to be precise]

Many years ago, before human beings searched the stars for new beings to fight, there was enough fighting to be done on planet earth. Many capital cities are filled with the monuments to those who died in one heroic struggle or another but across Europe you will see many statues of Charlotte the Liberator.

Given that so much of our lives are spent being monitored by CCTV, followed online or listened to on the phone, it seems incredible that no-one is completely sure when Charlotte was born. We know that it was in the M & J Holdings Hospital in a small semi-rural Welsh village and that her parents had to claim on their insurance for the cost of the visit. We would then assume that Charlotte would have disappeared into the kind of ordinary life that fills up the boxes of data that no-one ever looks at in the National Records archive.

Charlotte was certainly unremarkable at school, her reports showing that she enjoyed art, IT and some sport but failing at the food technology and customer service courses that were the main offering at the McDonald's Academy. Her teachers found her interesting and bright, but not exceptional. However, our first glimpse of our hero's extraordinary talents does come when she is shown the timetables for lessons for those around the age of sixteen. In an incident as famous now as anything done by a young George Washington or Winston Churchill, Charlotte asked the school secretary why she did not print the timetables for each class on different coloured paper to make them easier to file. I think that you can see already some of that spirit that would earn all those statues.

The Careers Computer at the Academy offered Charlotte few choices. Like all her fellow students, Charlotte entered a list of her skills and qualifications and the computer told her what she was worth. She could then match that to a list of roles available to someone of her age and background to find out her career. Her lack of a pass on the customer service module held her back, even though she had explained to a tutor that her failure to complete the work was because she was caring for her mother who had fallen ill.

Luckily for our hero, one of her teachers at the Academy who had found the colour-coded timetables much easier to understand had recently moved to the Ford Motor Cars School in Bridgend and had recommended Charlotte when a job had become available in the school office. It is here that she earned the name that most people knew her by for the rest of her life : Charlotte the Administrator.

Charlotte soon understood that the 'paperless office' policy of the school meant that everything had to be kept on paper and on computer as well. She worked to match the folders on the computer with the folders on the shelves so that administrators could find information and switch between the two systems easily.

She introduced a spreadsheet for recording stock leaving the stationery cupboard and created an automatic re-ordering system so that the school never ran out of supplies. Her spreadsheets – some of which are preserved in national museums to this day (though some, it has been argued, are fake) – were so well-regarded that she was awarded with a 'Queen of the Spreadsheets' mug and became a well-regarded person for management requests for supplies.

We know that she was a popular employee in the school and that she dated as any attractive young woman might, but that her life was somewhat constricted by supporting her mother, who had stopped working due to ill-health. Others were shocked that Charlotte gave some of her earnings to pay for her mother's care and questioned why her mother had not saved from an early age for such an eventuality but perhaps it is a sign of our hero's character that she did this.

Indeed, maybe it is a sign of why she made her next surprising move. The Channel 6 documentary maker Ladislau Heron had taken a trip to Bridgend to film a programme about poverty and how surprisingly costly it was. Intrigued by the mention of Charlotte's story and her unusual activity in looking after her mother during illness, he asked to meet her. All Charlotte knew was that Channel 6 had just won the rights to show football highlights and she might be able to obtain tickets for Cardiff City matches from the stranger from London. After all, everything – even a chance meeting – has a financial value.

Ladislau Heron made our hero a surprising offer. He had been asked to keep an eye out for a potential female host for their football highlights show and listening to Charlotte talk about Cardiff City FC made him wonder if maybe he had found someone. After a couple of meetings, he asked her how she would feel about spending weekends in London and also if she would mind having her hair dyed blonde and wearing leather trousers on camera.

Charlotte the Administrator was not exactly pleased about the latter conditions and asked if they were not rather sexist. Ladislau Heron was not impressed by this question and explained to her that Channel 6 could not be accused of any kind of sexism as half of their presenters were female and was he not there offering her a job? He would later admit that it was Charlotte's irrational stroppiness about being told to look good on camera that convinced him that she had the temperament to be a star.

The money on offer was considerable and given that Charlotte the Administrator had never even been able to afford the cost of a train ticket to London, it seemed a way that she could move on and help pay her mother's bills.

Our hero's time as a presenter of Channel 6's football highlights show is well-known to some readers. She would arrive in London on a Saturday and go to hair and make-up as well as being fitted in to new clothes. The wardrobe department tended to favour low-cut tops and leather trousers plus her hair was always carefully dyed. Once prepared, her job was to sit to the right of her co-presenter Danny, smile and throw easy questions to Managers like, "Do you think that your team can survive the season?". Danny meanwhile would talk tactics and strategy with the professionals.

Charlotte liked Danny. He was supposed to be the cute, bloke next door who the viewer could share a pint with and talk tactics. He had a fashionable beard and a collection of slightly formal waistcoats. What the viewers were supposed to think of Charlotte she was less than clear, though Danny kindly instructed the media department to remove the death threats and the more extreme sexual requests from the messages that were sent to her.

This may seem a strange detour for our hero on the way from being Charlotte the Administrator to becoming Charlotte the Liberator. Yet it was her friendship with Danny that was to make a crucial difference to the direction of her life.

Danny was fun. He had great sympathy for Charlotte and the way that she had to arrive so much earlier than him in the studio. He was more likely to turn up in his own clothes and only need a little bit of work from hair and make up. He agreed that it was not completely fair that she never had the tactical questions to ask and once let her ask something about the offside strategy of Norwich City FC, even though he knew that the producer would tell him off for doing so. Being seen by millions of people every week is an isolated existence and the exciting world of television is quite often boring, so the two would spend time chatting while waiting for their cue. One time Danny told Charlotte that she looked better when she arrived at the studio than when she emerged prepared for the cameras.

Some of Charlotte's background did become useful. She showed one director how to organise his notes and running order better to manage the flow of the programme. She introduced a washing up rota for the studio kitchen and overhauled the expenses system so that payments did not build up until the end of the month. She was popular, the programme was liked by viewers and Charlotte's mother's care was being paid for.

One night, Charlotte asked Danny to go to a pub with her for a drink. They enjoyed chatting together and making fun of the ever-changing rota of directors who told them where to sit and how to talk. Danny was still getting more marriage proposals than she was, but as each drink was ordered, they seemed to find more in common. Both of them were aware that not just CCTV but online newspapers would be following their every move and so when Charlotte mentioned that she had a bottle of fine whisky back at the flat that Channel 6 was paying for in London, Danny agreed to move on with her for the next drink.

Back at her flat, Charlotte poured the drinks and made her move. She snuggled in to the sofa and when Danny seemed to have paused in his thoughts on the latest advice on how long interviews with ex-Managers should last, she leaned in and kissed him firmly on the lips. It seemed the most normal and natural and sensible thing to do and it would have been a glorious moment in our hero's life but for the fact that Danny pushed her off and said 'Ugh!'

Future liberator of oppressed peoples or not, it never feels good when you kiss someone and they say 'ugh!' Danny was quick to apologise and explain that he was gay. He produced a picture of a clean-cut looking man from his wallet and said that this was Ed and that the two were very happy together. Channel 6 still sent out press releases saying that he was eligible and available to female fans, but he was very much not available. He also thought that she looked better as a brunette.

Charlotte was taken aback of course and felt foolish but Danny stayed long enough to re-assure her. Even the photos on social media the next day of him leaving her flat at midnight were not that hard to laugh off the next day in work. The publicity department were very pleased with all the attention on their two stars and Danny had a congratulatory message from them asking him to keep them informed as to how the relationship was progressing.

The next week, Danny asked Charlotte to return to his flat after work. Ed was out and he wanted to explain a few things to her, things that she might not know having come from a small Welsh town. Charlotte was unsure of what to expect of the encounter and at first it was just a drink and a chat about how they had handled the debate on safe standing in football grounds.

Then Danny's tone changed : "When I first met you, I wondered if you were a management plant. I know that they spy on us and you looked like a ... well, you looked like someone who did not belong here. You were too intelligent, you knew too much about sport, I saw you analyse something about passing play and yet ... yet, you were happy to sit there and ask the inane questions to some ex-Charlton Athletic manager who was on the show because he could not get a proper job. It didn't make sense."

Charlotte knew that she lived in a society monitored by CCTV and where every online interaction was stored and analysed but she always believed what she had been told as a child, that this was important to protect the country. That her own employers would spy on her seemed new, but she simply nodded and let Danny talk further.

"It was last week that changed my mind. If the government has a file on me, then surely they have Ed in it. We keep it quiet but my goodness people must know. It's not like I could be blackmailed, people aren't judgemental like that now thank goodness, but it will affect my image, especially in football which is a bit slow to catch up with society. If you were spying on me, you would not have tried for a drunken snog."

"Thanks for reminding me," mused Charlotte, idly swishing the wine in her wine glass back and forth and not making eye contact with him.

"There is a different world there, a different society. When I was coming out ... it was pretty hard even with less judgement ... but I had support from a group who are part of what is called 'the third sector'. I can tell from your face that you have never heard of them. They help people ... for free."

Charlotte laughed at the absurdity, "Everything has a price, we learned that at school. Nothing comes for free - my mother's care, you should see the cost of that! We had insurance when I was born, of course, but ..."

Danny looked at her intensely and grabbed her arm a little too tightly, "It's true. It exists. People give their time for free - they volunteer."

Charlotte shook her head now, "Volunteering? I remember that - when you are unemployed, that's what the Job Centre make you do if you want benefits."

"No!" insisted Danny, gripping Charlotte's arm so tightly that she made a small yelp and pulled it away from him, "Take this card. It has a number on it, it's the nearest place I could find to your home. Don't get caught with it, doing stuff for free goes against everything you've learnt about society, no-one wants you to know that it is possible."

Charlotte took the card and placed it cautiously into her bag. It seemed to be an address and some numbers in Swansea This did not make any sense to her but Danny seemed so grateful to these people that she felt that she ought to contact them, if only for him.

The funny thing was that the more she thought about it, the more she understood it. The conversation and the wine and whisky continued to flow but in the back of her mind she had returned to a question that had occurred to her before - what would have happened to her mother if she had not been able to pay her hospital bills?

"What now?" she asked.

"Now we build an alibi. If you haven't realised, there are social media cameras outside and those who are not there will be buying the CCTV images from the cameras across the street. I am eighty-nine percent sure that I am not being bugged yet. At about three a.m., I suggest that you leave here. You need to smear your lipstick, ruffle your dress as if it has been pulled on hurriedly and mess up your hair a bit. Say nothing to the camera crews but smile shyly all the way to the taxi. Believe you me, no-one will be asking if we have discussed radical politics."

Danny was not wrong and Charlotte smiled when she saw the online newspapers the next day - Channel 5's hottest couple had 'shared a night of passion', apparently. Charlotte's shy smile and reticence on leaving convinced waiting journalists that the two had taken part in a 'steamy encounter'. 'Three a.m. Walk of Shame!' screamed one newspaper, accompanied by speculation as to what her appearance meant about what had taken place in Danny's flat.

However, she had escaped London and headed back to Wales. The timing was fortunate, she was already booked to shoot an advert for Harrison's Carpets in Bridgend and it would be a short journey from there on to the address on the card - 'Orchard House' in Swansea. Channel 6's top presenter buys her carpets from Harrison's. This was the stuff that local advertising was made from but it paid bills back home.

She had been to many of the pubs and restaurants in the city, but she had never heard of Orchard House. Indeed, when she saw Orchard House she knew why - it was a run-down 1960s office block that was surely soon to be demolished. A phone call to the number on the card and a brief discussion about how she had got hold of it led to being told to enter '1,3,7,9' into the door security and to ask for Schwartzkopf Hair Care, office number eight.

Our hero had decided to pose as her less glamorous sister Helen if anyone recognised her. However, the chaos of the small eight feet by eight feet office amazed her. There were no desks, no computers and no filing cabinets, let alone any weaponry for a revolutionary fight. There were seven or eight staff buzzing around but they were concentrating on taking up the old, moth-eaten carpet. Any thought of being her lesser-known sister disappeared as Charlotte stepped over the rolled-up end of the carpet and put a call through to Harrison's. A new carpet was installed within the day as a thank you to their star.

Having identified herself through her connections, Charlotte sat down with Leanne the Manager. Leanne had been working behind the scenes for many years on a range of projects that Charlotte had never heard of - projects to stop young people dropping out of education, projects to combat loneliness among older people, projects to improve the environment. What she simply could not understand is why they did all these things for no money. The Careers Computer back at school would never have recommended that you wasted your skills for so little reward. There were paid staff but they all could have been earning more in any of the local companies.

Leanne had a beguiling utopia though. A country where people accepted that a healthy population benefited everyone, where everyone had a chance to show their talents regardless of wealth, a country where the poorest were cared for and people supported while looking for work. Charlotte did not have to think about her mother for long before realising that this really was a better world.

Leanne had a vision, what she did not have was a filing system. Everyone in that office was a Project Manager and no matter that Leanne said that funding cuts always take out administration and that it was very hard to raise money for an underground movement, Charlotte the Administrator recognised her calling.

Charlotte the Administrator continued to live her triple life. In London at the weekend she was Channel 6's glamorous presenter who the newspapers followed and photographed everywhere she went. She and Danny had fun staging arguments and break-ups as speculation swerved from whether they were about to become engaged to whether it was over. No-one for a minute suspected that she was anything other than the blonde one from the football highlights show.

She would also do adverts and media appearances and talks in schools about how hard work would get you where you wanted to be, even though she knew that that was a lie and that anyone at McDonald's Academy was already losing out to anyone at Eton. She played the game as well as any of the professionals whose passing skills were analysed by Danny every Saturday night.

All the rest of her time was spent with 'the third sector'. She introduced Gantt charts and project plans. She wanted to do lists for everyone and spreadsheets that showed the actions to be taken, their cost and when they would take place. Spreading the idea of a better life, one where people saw value beyond something financial was done one village and one town at a time. However, each operation had a folder and each folder was subdivided into different categories so that any time it was known what was happening throughout the sector.

Slowly the revolution grew. There was a lot of resistance of course, but the majority of people were waiting for someone to tell them that their life was worth more than the Careers Computer said it was worth. People were encouraged to learn things, to do things, to make things just for the fun of it and who cared if it never made any money? It was freedom and well, you know the society that we built as a result.

None of this would have been possible without good administration and this is why in every city liberated by this new idea, there is now a statue among the great and the good of Charlotte the Liberator. Each one shows her in her most heroic pose - looking upwards to a better future, laptop in one hand, spreadsheet in another. On the pedestal is one simple teaching of the Liberator -

"The revolution will not be televised but it will need an efficient filing system."

From Wow to Ow

You have to sit on the left hand side of the train.

When I started catching the train from here every morning, there were only about ten people on the platform. They would arrive, right on cue, with a minute to spare and we would jump on to the train together. It is much busier now, there must be fifty or sixty people huddled into their winter coats in the morning, their breath visible and their intent to get a seat for themselves and their bag clear.

You have to sit on the left hand side of the train, though.

Getting a table does not matter and, let us be frank, the civil servants who get on at the next stop will probably want 'their' table. You can try sitting there, but they will look at you as if you have stolen it from them or, even worse, they will talk to you.

No, a table is not important, sitting on the left hand side of the train is important.

The students make a difference. In the winter, they stand in the corridors, laugh loudly and seem joyful about the possibilities of the day ahead while the adults stare into their coffee or free newspaper. In the summer the students disappear, yet still most people getting on the train a few stops after mine will struggle to find a seat. As soon as the students leave the station, they huddle together in a fog of cigarette smoke and stride out into the road as if they do not have to care because the traffic will always stop for them.

The students never worry about which side of the train they are lounging on.

The teenagers are funny too. Some of them go to school using this line. There was a girl the other day telling her friend about how annoyed she was that her Dad was 'staying over'. He lived down the other end of the street and she was okay with him calling in to see her and her Mum, but she hated having to share the bathroom the next morning. 'Why can't he just go home to his own house at night?' she was demanding of her friend. They will learn.

I moved after my marriage ended. You will be able to see where I lived in a few stops' time. I enjoyed being married but it came to an end and I am not someone who lets past things affect how they live now. You have to move on, as my ex-wife did while we were still married.

I like the architecture from the left hand side of the train. This next stop, there is a lovely, old Victorian house built in the middle of that nineteenth century explosion of confidence. For them, everything was possible and their buildings reflected that. It is a good view from the left hand side of the train.

In fact, this is probably the reason why I am so keen to sit here each day. That is, sit on the left on the way to work in the morning and on the right on the way back – though frankly, getting a seat on the way back is harder, so I sometimes just stand with my back to whatever is going on outside on that other side of the train. I am not interested in it, whatever it is.

I was devastated when my marriage broke up, I will admit that. I suppose that that is one of the reasons why I moved further away from work, something about trying to delete painful memories. New routines would make me happy all over again. I used to work on this database at work – 20,000 records all in one programme – and I spent hours working on it after my marriage broke up, staying on late into the night to do tedious, distracting work just to avoid dealing with the world and going home to a cold, empty house. That year I had a glowing appraisal and endless praise about my 'commitment to the company'.

My appraisals slid back to 'should work harder' when I met Diana. She was fabulous. It felt as though marriage had been one, long night out and I had been hungover since it ended, but Diana seemed to revitalise everything about me and make me feel sober again. She was fun and interesting and we had intelligent conversations about love and God and happiness and religion and anything you cared to name. We whispered conspiratorially about how the world was against us and we had to be a team to take it on. No-one else understood our little couple and the jokes that we could tell with a sideways glance or a raised eyebrow.

Up here is the river. You can only see it from this side of the train. I am not sure what happens on the other side, they may have filled it in or channelled it underground. On this side it is still flowing. It looks rather grey and forlorn on this winter's day, but it is there - if you are sitting on the left hand side of the train.

Diana left too. This is not self-pity. I wanted to talk to her about our feelings and it turned out that hers were not as strong as mine. She did the decent thing and ended it. There is no point dwelling on it, I decided to move on.

The train makes its final loop through some goods yards and then into its final stop. I will admit that this last part of the journey is a little dull over here on the left, as all you ever see are the queues of trains waiting to fit into a station too small for them. This is still the place to sit.

You have to sit on the left hand side of the train.

What else can I tell you about Diana? Nothing really, she came along and I felt happy again and knew that happiness was possible again. I should thank her for that.

As I say, I am not the kind of person who lets their past define their present. She lived around here, just before you reach the final station. You can see her house – from the right hand side of the train.

The Orange Hoodie

[This story started life as a challenge to write a variation on the 'evil babysitter' type of story. I also wanted to write a story viewed by two different female narrators. I feel though that I should add that I was brought up by a single mother and that the comments about single mothers in this story do not reflect my views]

Diane 1

When I first saw her, I thought that she was some kind of angel.

It may be hard to imagine what it is like to contemplate your first night out in years, but now I stood in the doorway to my flat looking at this woman who would make it all possible. Though I was standing there in baggy jeans and with scrambled egg on my oversized hoodie, my angel smiled at me and said hello, before her eyes dropped to look at the cause of all my problems. I could probably treat it as an advance in his development that there was more scrambled egg on him than on me.

"I'm Justine," my angel said and she scooped up the little monster from the floor into her arms and added, "and you must be Ben."

"The place is a bit of a mess …" I started as Justine carried Ben past me into the tiny room that functioned as sitting room, Ben's bedroom and playroom.

Justine waved an arm at me to say that it was no bother and I took a proper look at her for the first time. She looked a lot like me, to be honest. We were the same height, the same curvy build and although her skin was lighter than mine and her hair an undyed mousy brown as opposed to my dyed dark brown, she looked like me … or perhaps a me who was not a single mother to a little tyrant. Her clothes were fitted and casual and without a trace of scrambled egg … so far.

"It's all right," she said, "you leave me and Ben to tidy up, you go get ready."

She looked at Ben as she said this, so I thought that I ought to give him a motherly kiss on the forehead as I walked passed them. He looked rather nonplussed and for a moment I thought that he would cry.

My bedroom was a mess and I did not even know where to start in terms of going out clothes. I had not been to a salsa night in years and all my clothes seemed to have had some stains or smells to remind me of some little accident of being a mother. I opened the wardrobe, a feat in itself as the door banged against the side of the bed, and looked in there.

I had not noticed her come in behind me but a voice said, "That dress right at the back, that's a dancing dress!"

"It's years since I wore that …" I started but Justine, still holding Ben to her side, nudged me and told me that it was my turn to go out and live a little.

I pulled out the dress and realised that it was more daring than anything I had worn for a long time, cut across the top to show one shoulder, a fairly cheeky sight of leg across the hem. She was right, I had not asked to be a single mother and why could I not enjoy myself just this once? I pulled it out of the wardrobe and waited for Justine to leave. She did not do so, so I indicated towards the door until she took the hint.

As I changed, I heard her ask through the door, "It's great that you get a chance to go out. You may be a Mum but you're a human-being too."

I agreed – how could I not agree – and added, "Well, his Dad was no help. Moment I was pregnant he was miles away. It's been me on my own since then."

"Does he help with the child support?" came the voice through the door.

At that moment I had been searching for clean underwear of any kind of decent type but the question made me stop. Justine was a friend of a friend recommended after I had made an anguished plea on a WhatsApp group to just have one night off being a full-time childminder. It seemed that she was being intrusive. I felt embarrassed and, as I pulled myself into the dress and hoped that the baby weight would not show, answered for fear of seeming rude.

"He has an evil accountant who fixes his tax returns to make it look like he has no money. Tosser. I've thought of putting a fist in his bloody face many times!"

"The accountant or the ex?"

"Both. But mainly the accountant. Charles was an arsehole but I did at least choose him. The accountant is one of those bloody men who enables others to screw you around."

I paused for breath and allowed myself to calm down. I had felt my whole body tensing and it was not good for me. I had my hair and make-up to do yet. Thank goodness the dress fitted.

The door opened.

"Wow!" said Justine, "you already look glam!"

"Thank you," I said, not entirely convinced.

"Ben and I will have a good time too while you are out, don't you worry about us."

I was amazed at how quickly Ben had taken to this stranger. Perhaps it was because she looked like me or perhaps it was just the calm energy she radiated. She was an angel, all right.

It was not long before a basic hair and make-up job had been completed and a bus ride into the city took me to the salsa club where I used to dance when I was free. I was still young, but that was the problem. The club would be filled with women my age, all into their first job with their disposable incomes or swapping stories of what university had been like. I was a single mother with a small child who stopped her going anywhere other than to buy nappies and toys.

Looking around the dark club, I felt my body sway to the music that I had not heard in years. I remembered coming here with Charles, wild and crazy nights out and then sharing a kebab on the night bus home. I remembered stumbling into the bedroom with him at the end of the night too, stupidly I still had the double bed in that pokey little room where the wardrobe would not open properly ... and the central heating kept me awake as it failed to work properly ... and the taps all dripped ... and the landlord said that he would re-attach the back door so it did not bang in the wind but he never did ... and ... and the looks of the women in the supermarket when Ben cried and they thought what a bad mother I was. They were right as well and that was why I ordered a double shot of tequila and decided that it was time to bloody party. Justine was my liberating angel and I was free for one night. If only it could be forever!

I stayed and danced far longer than I expected. My body remembered the rhythms but my energy was lost. I had exercised to get the baby weight off, but I was still unused to hours of movement and sometimes I lost my breath. Men twirled me around and I stepped as best as I could in time with the music and their moves. It was heavenly, but exhausting.

How often did I check my phone? How often did I ring Justine to ask how my son was doing? You know what we mothers are like, minds never quite on being out of the house when there is a child to worry about. Not me, I knocked back tequila like it was about to run out and enjoyed every twirl and every spin. Justine was looking after Ben, why should I worry?

Staggering back through town once the club had closed, I stopped to catch my breath and realised that I was opposite the office of Lomax and Lomax, Bastards. The sign actually said Lomax and Lomax, Accountants but I swayed backwards and stuck two fingers up at them with such force that I took a couple of drunken steps back. That was for all the women who had been cheated out of child support by money-grabbing accountants advising ex-husbands!

"Fuck you!" I shouted, now sticking two sets of V-signs up at them, "Fuck fuckfuck you and all your fucking fucking fuckwits! Fuck you!"

Swearing in public felt liberating until I worried that they had CCTV cameras pointing at me. I walked unsteadily forwards and peered in the window. No-one inside and only a sign advertising a vacancy for an administrator stuck to the window. Well, if there was a CCTV camera then what would I care? They had the message!

When I arrived home, I would not say that Justine gave me a look that said 'what time do you call this, young Madam?' but it felt very much for a moment like my mother was telling me off, with a silent point to the front room to remind me that a child was asleep in there. I apologised and took off my shoes as quietly as I could. This meant falling over and hitting the wall. Justine caught me. In fact, she held me steady and walked me to the bedroom, where I fell straight on to the bed with a crumpled, muffled thud.

"I need to be going," said Justine uncertainly.

"Don't go!" I said a little too loudly and then moderated back to a quieter voice, "don't go!"

Justine laughed and I was not sure if she was enjoying my drunkenness or mocking me.

"You only have one bedroom and I can't sleep with the boy. No, don't worry, I live in Roath, I can walk across town. It's no bother."

I sat up and spread a hand across my double bed.

"Sleep with me," I said, "you know, sisterly like. I've got a bed big enough for two. It's no problem."

"Are you sure?" she asked.

"I've got a spare toothbrush in the bathroom," I added, "just …"

"I guess it would be useful for if Ben wakes …" pondered Justine.

However, by this time I had climbed into bed fully-clothed, pulled the covers over me and drifted off to sleep. I had a vague memory of someone closing the doors, switching the lights off, putting me in the recovery position and then climbing in bed next to me. I felt her warmth. She was an angel.

Justine 1

When I first saw her, I thought that she was some kind of demon.

She wore the worst, most unflattering clothes and they were covered in scrambled egg. She lived in this pokey little flat in a run-down part of Adamsdown, but she had this gorgeous young man by her side. I had always wanted a child of my own and though biologically I could keep waiting for another ten or maybe fifteen years, there was something about seeing this mother devote herself to raising this child that was awe-inspiring. That I could help her look after him while she took time to enjoy herself was a privilege.

However, she was so tired and clumsy and dowdy that I thought that she must have had some spell on her blinding her to the wonderful life that she had. What an awesome thing it would be to be a single mother, I thought.

Ben took to me immediately, which was wonderful. I did notice that I looked a lot like his mother, though my hair was a different colour and I thought that my face was a slightly different shape. Still we were the kind of people who you would confuse for each other if you saw one of them in the supermarket. It only made me warm to her more and more.

I had been shown the plea she made on the WhatsApp Group and, to be honest, it was not as if my life had been exciting before then. University was proving a drag and although my own little flat in Roath was no paradise, I yearned to be the kind of grown-up who owned their own toaster. The neverending round of lectures, fees, parties and study groups was not exactly lucrative and so being paid to look after a little boy, especially one who was so cute, seemed good.

I say that Diane looked like a demon, but I was being unfair. She looked as though the world had beaten her down. I am not sure if it was her ex- or the poverty or the stress, but she looked as though she was weary of it all. As soon as I saw her, I knew that I could help. I felt drawn to her, perhaps because she looked like me, but a version of me who was messing up parenting. That is why I knew that she had to go out and have a good time that night.

I will admit that i was not expecting her back at half two in the morning reeking of booze and covered in sweat. Still less was I expecting to be invited to sleep with her. I did have a temptation to say something like 'I'm into tall, dark men who know how to wear a shirt' but she was drunk and I thought of that small child needing his Mummy, so I stayed. It was more interesting than anything else in my life at that moment.

Diane 2

I was so hungover the next day. I was not used to tequila and my head just throbbed. At first, I had this idea of giving Ben colouring to do or something to keep him quiet, but my angel Justine was on the case while I was still placing a pillow over my head in the hope that its smoothness would somehow make me feel less rough.

She made breakfast for Ben, even bringing me some mashed-up Weetabix to stare at in case my stomach felt kinder. Then I could hear them watching television together and playing with bricks or something. Not real bricks, toy bricks but I suppose that you knew that. I was soon to realise that Justine was an innovator, always trying to think of new ways to entertain the little monster and nearly always succeeding.

I had post-natal depression after he was born. I remember it like it was a vague kind of dream now, but I remember a feeling of revulsion towards Ben and then fear that I would actually hurt him. I was supposed to bond with him and there were relatives desperate to tell me how wonderful and life-affirming motherhood would be.

Charles had left before I gave birth and so he was no help. My parents sided with him and thought I 'shouldn't have let him go', as if I could have chained him to the sink when he decided that getting me pregnant was a deal-breaker in our relationship. I used to visit them quite often but when I heard one of my Dad's friends saying that there would be 'less single mothers if some of these girls kept their legs together', I decided not to bother again. This is why I thought that it was mad that Justine wanted to be a single mother.

However, this was nothing to do with post-natal depression now. I was not depressed, I was balanced and 'normal' and happy and I did not want to be a mother. I knew that I was not supposed to feel like this- possibly not allowed to - but going out the night before had reminded me what motherhood had taken away from me.

My angel Justine continued to look after Ben while I recovered from my hangover and so I suggested the next day that we popped up to Roath. We could take Ben to Roath Park and then go and get some clothes and other possessions from Justine's house. I wasn't asking her to move in, I just wanted my angel to give me some time off from being a full-time Mum and more time as what I thought to be a normal twenty-five year old.

Justine was okay about this, but she worried about where the money would come from. She was right and as we played in Roath Park that day, I did wonder what we could do to prolong this situation. I watched Justine play in the park with Ben and I listened to the other mothers talk about the usual things to do with nappies and playgroups and the pain of standing on Lego.

Justine took Ben to see the monument to Scott of the Antarctic and prattled on about exploration or something, even though he was far too young to understand. I suppose that she was not good at everything.

When it came time for Justine to go back to her flat to collect some things, I tried playing with Ben myself. When he ran off, one of the other mothers caught him and brought him back to me with the words, "Do you want to go back to your Auntie? I'm sure your Mum will be back soon." When she reached me she said, "Your sister's lucky to have such a lovely boy!"

I sulked on the journey home. It was a full-on, not looking at you, grumpy, you know what you have done sulk which lasted all the way home. For all that I was grateful for this woman coming into my life, I did also resent the easy way that she had taken on the mothering role which I had struggled with for these last few years. I did not like being replaced. Still, being a single mother had taught me to be adaptable and maybe that was what needed to happen, I needed to find a new role. If I wanted money for going out and she wanted money for looking after the child, perhaps there was a solution.

That night once Ben was in bed, I opened a bottle of wine and said to Justine, "I want to get a job."

Justine 2

Yeah, I loved being with Ben and I thought that it was a joy to be a mother to him. However, I only ever saw it as a short-term thing at first. I was having so much fun with him and, of course, with Diane, that when she suggested I moved some of my things into her flat, I was happy to go along with it. I did not have many things and so a temporary move would be fine. We could both look after Ben and that little man would get two single Mums.

The day we went to Roath Park was a little odd. To be honest, I think that Diane was still a little hungover. She spent most of the day staying quiet while I played with Ben. We went to look at the Scott Monument in the park and I told him all about the bravery and the adventure of the Antarctic explorers. He was far too young to understand any of it, of course, but I thought that telling him all about these things now might help build his curiosity in the world. I wanted him to grow to think about exploration and the wonder of the world himself.

After I had filled some bags of clothes and stuff back at my flat, Diane seemed in a really odd mood with me. Perhaps one of the other mothers had pointed out something that I was doing wrong in my childminding, but she sulked all the way back to the flat. It really was a sulk too, silent, angry and contemptuous. Had she been a child I would have sent her to bed without any dinner until she apologised.

The idea of her getting a job threw me at first, to be honest. Yeah, I had asked about where the money would come from to support the three of us, but I only meant in terms of an extra mouth to feed in the home while I was there. I had wondered if she had wanted a contribution from me so when she said that she wanted to go back to work, well, I was unsure what to say. She had once been a Civil Servant, quite a capable one at that I think, so finding a new job would be no trouble but I was not sure about her going out to work all day and leaving me on my own. Drinking wine with her helped calm my nerves.

Maybe this tension was building because when we decided to celebrate her new job (secured on the first interview she went for – I told you, this woman was amazing) we ended up having our first huge argument. Diane wanted to go to her salsa class and have a big night out but I pointed out that that meant that I could not celebrate with her. I wanted to celebrate, but it seemed selfish to leave me with Ben again while she was out partying. I asked her if she remembered the time that she had staggered home at half two in the morning and then added, 'oh hold on, you'd be too pissed out your head to remember'.

There was some shouting, some slamming of doors and Ben crying – frankly, if it was the kind of neighbourhood where people gave a damn, then Social Services would have been called. However, the storm faded as quickly as it had blown up and we agreed that she would go out on Friday night for a small celebration and then come home once Ben was safely tucked up in bed and share a bottle of wine with me.

I am pleased to say that she did exactly as she was told and that night we sat on the bed together and knocked back wine – I had already drunk about half the bottle before she came home so we were both drunkenly laughing quietly and talking about everything. I had friends at university, but she was my big sister, my mate, my confidante, my mentor and the woman I admired. Soon I was asking her the kind of things friends at University had talked about late at night in tiny student flats which were never cleaned.

"So, what's the best sex you've ever had?" I asked, trying to point at her but possibly just pointing at the wardrobe behind her.

Diane laughed and took another swig of wine.

"Oh Charles. Charles, Charles, Charles every time. We had ... you know when you see someone and you just want to jump straight into bed with them? Maybe we were doomed as a couple but oh my goodness, the chemistry. I couldn't get enough of him and if that little monster hadn't come along, who knows ... who knows ..."

I smiled at her honesty. I wished that I could be like her even more now.

"He really fucked you into next week, then?" I asked.

Diane had obviously never heard the phrase before and frowned at me, before having to put a hand out to stop herself falling over on to the bed, glass in hand. For some reason frowning had disrupted her ability to balance. Maybe it was the swearing. I realised that she never swore.

"You never heard that expression?" I asked, "Think it's great. You know where you have such good sex that you are kind of walking around for a few days in a zombie-like state thinking of nothing else. That's being fucked into next week."

Diane repeated the phrase and it sounded odd on her lips but I liked the sound of her voice. She sounded just that little bit posher than me and she formed her words with a little bit more care and dedication. I knew that I wanted to sound like that too so I repeated the phrase in her voice. She laughed at me and I had to 'ssh!' her again to remind her that Ben was asleep in the next room. This only made her laugh more.

"I do not sound like that!" she protested when the laughing had subsided.

"I do not sound like that!" I repeated, mirroring her every syllable.

"Creepy," she said and I poured her some more wine.

I admired her, that was all. I wanted to be like her and so I had to learn how she behaved, how she sounded, how she looked, how to be Diane Morgan.

Diane 3

It was the orange hoodie that changed everything. I had let Justine into my home as a babysitter and I had been initially glad of her staying, but seeing her in my orange hoodie sent me in a whole different direction.

It was not that I loved the hoodie, although it was warm and dependable. It was not that it was one of the few things left over from when I was dating Charles, it was simply that it made me realise that I had spent a few weeks with this woman in my flat, playing with my son, washing up my dishes and tidying everything up around me. A little of that resentment that had welled up in me at Roath Park came to the surface again.

I had come home early, I admit that. It was my home though and walking into my bedroom to see her standing there in my orange hoodie almost made me want to scream.

"Where did you get that?" I demanded.

"Oh no, it's yours, not mine," she replied with an airy confidence as if I had forgotten where it was bought rather than that it was mine.

Then I looked down and saw Ben looking up at her in it. He looked calm and quiet and re-assured. These were not words I thought of when he was around me. Did he not deserve better than a mother who was constantly stressed and hassled and overtaken with a burning dislike of his father? What if this woman standing there so brazenly in my hoodie was that better version of me, that one who actually liked children? Maybe that was what her arrival had done, it had liberated me from having to be the mother figure who I struggled to be? She kept saying that she admired me for being a single mother, for taking on the responsibility on my own (forgetting that I had no choice in the matter) and looking at me as if I was some kind of superwoman. Maybe she could be the helper in the project.

I know that I should have seen her as a crazy stalker trying to replace me, but having a friend who was such a help made a difference to me. The average age to have your first child in this country is thirty. That meant that my friends were all partying still and had long ago become bored of the friend who was never free to come out and when she did, only talked about nappies and feeding. Was she trying to replace me? It hardly mattered when I had a new best friend.

From then on we started to make everything a bit more formal. I let her share my wardrobe and even sent her out to do shopping for our clothes. I still wanted to be a crazy young woman who went for nights out, so we bought going out clothes and then dressed up in the bedroom together, knocking back wine but never actually going out. I will admit that I liked her getting the cheapest and tackiest clothes for herself from Primark. Perhaps I wanted to look down on her a bit. Then again, she was in her mid-twenties and already had a young son to look after, some people would have been judgemental about that.

We shared everything over wine. I told her that I was still in love with Charles and she talked about loneliness. We joked about being twins and I gave her my ID so she could open a bank account. I know what you are thinking, I gave my crazy stalker twin my ID, but I took hers as safety and it seemed reasonable that she had a bank account to use for household expenses. If I was going to be out at work, I needed to be paying into it so she never needed to wonder where the shopping bill was going to come from.

I did go to her flat in Roath a couple of times. I told her that I was going for job interviews each time and she never even noticed that her keys had gone. Why would she, she was so used to using mine? There was very little of value there. Her housemates seemed to be students who stayed for a few months of study before moving on. They had heard rumours about the woman whose door was always locked and although I thought that the explanation that she had summoned demons that had destroyed part of the Adult Education Centre was amusing, I told them that she had had a baby and been made to drop out. She was keeping the room for when she returned. So long as she kept paying her rent, no-one was going to ask questions.

However, I suppose that it would be right to say that we passed that summer having fun together, drinking once Ben was asleep, playing crazy games and Justine looking after the child while I had nights out. Sometimes she gave me that look of 'what time do you call this, young Madam?' again when I returned drunk, but it never lasted long.

Perhaps I should have seen her in my orange hoodie and thought that she was a crazy stalker trying to steal my life but it was the orange hoodie that changed everything. It was the moment that I had a plan.

Justine 3

It was the orange hoodie that changed everything. I will admit that I should never have put it on but it was a cold day and I did feel a little guilty. However, I think that it was when she saw me in it that Diane realised that I could be a good mother for Ben and she could have more of the life that she wanted. We could be a good team.

Before she found me that day, I had been cleaning up our bedroom with Ben toddling around. It was cold and I had not wanted to put the heating on. The trouble was that with many of my clothes still in Roath, I had little to choose from. Looking into Diane's wardrobe, I saw an orange hoodie that looked so snug that I just had to take it out.

"Mummy!" Ben had called and I could not resist saying, "That's me!" in reply but he cried.

Then I put on the orange hoodie and, going for even more of a prompt for him, I sprayed some of Diane's favourite perfume on myself. Now Ben tugged at my leg and said, "Mummy! Mummy!"

I sat down on the bed and pulled him up on to my knee. We looked in the mirror together. But for the hair and the skin tone, I really was very similar to his mother and now with Ben sitting on my knee, I really could be his mother.

"It's all right," I said to him, "Mummy's here."

I'd only just stood up again when Diane arrived home early and found me in the hoodie. I think that it was the moment that we became best friends. Perhaps she had looked in a mirror too and thought that we could be sisters.

We had so much fun after that. I moved in properly. We no longer had a wardrobe which I occasionally used, it was our wardrobe. We shared our clothes. Diane became like a big sister to me and dyed my hair using her hair dye and then showed me how to do make-up like she did it. We had great sisterly bonding sessions where we would get dressed up in the bedroom after Ben had gone to sleep and knock back wine while trying to stop each other giggling.

Diane would sometimes give me things to buy from the clothes shops. She turned out to have quite trashy tastes, which surprised me. We were the same size, so

I would buy things and then we would get dressed up together - I remember the trashiest outfit she put on me was a see-through leopard print top with no bra underneath, a thigh-length black leather skirt, fishnet tights and black, high-heeled shoes. She then did shocking red nails and lips, with some over-the-top make-up to match.

"I look like a hooker!" I complained.

"Men will love it," she re-assured me and then got me to pose while she took some photos on her phone. Then we just fell about laughing looking at the pictures, especially as I was posing surrounded by empty wine bottles from our regular Wednesday night wine and pizza night.

It was not all me and her. My little angel was involved too - we went out to the backyard once and built a stone circle for him. We were in Wales, why not? Diane wore big gardening gloves and passed me these huge rocks (I wondered if she was testing how strong I was) and I mishandled them with awkward fingers and Ben patted them down into place.

I missed her when she went to work, but I had enough to do looking after Ben during the day. Money was tight and one day she suggested that we shared a bank account. We had been joking about how much alike we looked, so she challenged me to go into a bank with her passport and driving licence and open an account in her name. It worked like a charm! I had to memorise things like her mother's maiden name and her birthday, but we swapped wallets to give me practice in case the bank found me out.

I was over the moon with all this. I had started off wanting her life and now I had not only moved into her life, I was a part of it, a valued part of it. Diane was the most generous person I had ever met - when my phone disappeared, she simply gave me hers to use.

Diane 4

I have read magazine articles by feminists that claim that there is something called a sisterhood. There is no sisterhood. Justine and I were not sisters under the skin, she was not my sister from another mister and just because we had the same chromosome arrangement, it did not make us allies. There was no great bond that held us together as women.

I still felt that resentment I felt in Roath Park the first weekend. Now I understood that I did not resent her for taking my role, I resented her for being good at it. If Ben was going to have a bad mother, then I was going to be that bad mother. However, I also knew that if Justine walked out the door and never came back I would return to the scruffy, dowdy woman with scrambled egg over her clothes. I did not want to be her. If Justine idolised that woman then let her clean scrambled egg out of Ben's hair, I did not care.

I should have felt bad about abandoning Ben, I know, but you need to look at it from the point of view of what was best for him. If I got over my resentment - I could convince myself this was selfless even - then Justine provided him with a wonderful mother. I could provide some money, that seemed to be what I was good at.

I made my plan and I executed it perfectly. Justine and I became the best of friends and when I was drunk and she thought that I would not remember, she would tell me how much she loved our little family and did not want anyone else intruding on it. I admit that I encouraged it. I remember coming home from the gym one Saturday morning to find my lunch on the table and Justine and Ben sitting there with conspiratorial smiles about the mess in the kitchen. I laughed to myself because I realised that Justine had started out wanting to be a single mother and she had ended up becoming the dutiful wife.

It was not good enough for me though. I never lost sight of the plan. Every day at work, every pizza eaten with Justine, every glass of wine I poured into her, every drunken gossipy game of dressing up, every time I heard Justine get up in the night to see if Ben was all right, I made my plan.

I told Justine that I had to work late one Friday and pick up some files from the office. She looked at me innocently as I went out the back way from the house. I knew that it might be the last time that I saw either of them with an innocent expression, but I could not even bring myself to hug them. I shut the back door on my old life and knew that soon I would be free. You should have felt how hard my heart pumped at the thought!

Justine 4

Diane said that she had to nip out that Friday evening. It was a little odd, especially as she left through the backyard and she was dressed to go to her job, but I thought that she had probably been called in late. It is never easy for the working woman! Besides, I had time to play and watch television with my little angel. Ben was good as gold of course and we had fun.

Eventually he tired though and I put him to bed in the front room. I smiled at him through the darkness and ruffled his hair gently.

"Who's Mummy's brave little boy, then?" I asked him as I turned out the light.

Walking into the kitchen I found the loveliest of surprises. Diane had left a bottle of Jim Beam whisky on the kitchen table with a note that simply said 'Drink Me'. Ha! She was expecting us to put in an extra drunken night together and I did not take much persuasion to pour out a glass. What a life this was, I thought. My favourite woman at work, my favourite son in bed and a glass of whisky or two to help me wait in the bedroom for Diane's return.

I had been lying in bed in my pyjamas for a little while when there was an ugly rap on the front door. My first thought was that it would wake Ben so I hurried to the door and flung it open nervously. To my surprise, two police officers stood in front of me. One was a short woman with brown hair protruding in an unruly way from under her hat and the other was a large man who looked like he could have had a side job as a bouncer.

"Diane Morgan?" the woman asked.

"Who wants to know?" I demanded.

"Can we come in?" asked the man.

"Justine Frazer," I clarified for them.

The two of them looked around and I noticed that Diane was standing behind them. She nodded and all three walked into the kitchen. What the hell was going on? I suddenly started to feel strangely exposed in my pyjamas.

I tried ineffectively to hide the whisky bottle but I realised that both the police officers had seen it. I smiled awkwardly and then walked into a chair clumsily.

"I've a child asleep in the next room," I said.

"We know," replied the man, "I'm Constable Lewis and this is Constable Harris. We'd like to ask you a few questions about your whereabouts tonight, Ms Morgan."

His voice was calm but I was starting to feel under observation. I tried to look past him to Diane but she did not meet my gaze.

"What is this about?" I demanded again, "I've got a child asleep in here!"

The woman spoke now, perhaps also using a voice designed to calm down distressed suspects.

"A large rock was thrown through the window of Lomax & Lomax Accountants tonight, Ms Morgan and we believe that you may know something about it."

I sat down on the kitchen stool and shook my head. Why did they keep calling me 'Morgan'?

"Lomax & Lomax - they're the accountants who did her ex-'s accounts," I said, pointing at Diane, who was still lurking in the back of the kitchen as though it were alien territory.

"No," replied Constable Lewis, "Ms Frazer works at Lomax & Lomax as an administrator. She was working late tonight when she saw you smash the window and shout obscenities as part of your ongoing campaign against your ex."

"Diane! What are you saying?" I shouted, a little too loudly.

The police officers looked at each other and I realised that they now thought that I was arguing with myself.

"What ongoing campaign anyway?" I asked.

Lewis took out a small notebook, one which I am sure that he did not have to read from. He struggled with it slightly as it had been tucked in a pocket beneath a florescent yellow safety jacket. He read from a page.

"On the night of the 13th - that was last Wednesday night, I believe - you sent obscene messages and a picture to your ex-husband using WhatsApp," he read out in a monotone.

"What? No! Wednesday! That's our pizza and wine night. I was drunk probably but no, no messages."

Harris looked over at the bottle of whisky that I had tried to put behind the dishes.

"Drink often when you're in charge of a small child, do you?"

I went to contradict her, suddenly aware that my breath smelt of whisky too. I simply shook my head and said that I had no idea what they were talking about.

"Check her phone," said Diane.

Lewis held out his hand and I took the phone from the kitchen table and placed it there.

"It's not my phone!" I protested as he opened it up to find a picture of me showing as a screensaver, a picture I did not remember putting there.

It only took him a few finger swipes to find a WhatsApp group and he read it slowly. He clearly thought for a while about what he had found.

"I am going to read some of this to you, Ms Morgan, but I hope Ms Frazer that you will forgive me for some of the language used, I will gloss over it."

Both Diane and I said 'okay' at the name 'Ms Frazer' and I glared at her. She was not making eye contact back at me.

Constable Lewis read in a terrible monotone, "'Please come and eff me you sexy bastard. I want you to screw me till I scream'. You carry on like that, though if you are going to write 'you're so big' you need to use 'you are' rather than the possessive 'your' you use here. Still, bad grammar is not a crime!"

At this, the other three of them laughed but I had no energy for it.

"Is this you?" asked Lewis showing me a picture of me dressed in my trashiest clothes on all fours on the bed. There was an empty bottle of wine on the bed next to me. I knew what I looked like. I could not stand the deception any longer.

"Will you just listen to me you idiots!" I yelled, "I am not Diane Morgan! I am Justine Frazer! Stop calling me Diane! Please!"

My voice was so loud that it woke Ben and there were cries from behind the front room door. The two police officers looked at each other and knocked the door open. They flashed torches into the front room, which hardly helped calm Ben down. That cry was gut-wrenching and I pushed past them into the room and switched the light on.

"I'm so sorry I yelled, so sorry I yelled," I called out to him and he wobbled across the floor towards my leg crying "Mummy! Mummy!"

Constable Lewis shined a torch straight into my face and asked sarcastically, "I suppose that's not your child then, Ms Morgan?"

Ben and I sat in the kitchen crying. He was crying through fear, I was crying with desperation. Yet I could hear what they were saying just outside the door, even though the voices were low.

Diane was saying, "Look, she's in a bad way and I hate to see any woman struggle. Clearly she has a problem with her ex- but she's not a bad person. I am sure that the firm won't press charges so why don't you just give her a telling off. I'm sure that if you take her finger prints they will match with the rock that smashed the window and if you take a few mug shots, just so that she knows that you know her name and whereabouts ... I am sure that it can be sorted out."

"What about being a drunken parent?" asked Lewis.

Constable Harris shook her head, "We'll just give her a warning. Write it up in case it becomes a social services referral but I think that she is just struggling. You've been very helpful Ms Frazer, especially in such difficult circumstances."

"It really was no trouble," Diane was saying.

"Can we give you a lift anywhere while we take this one down to the station?" Lewis was asking.

"No, I live in Roath, I'll get a taxi back there," Diane replied.

As the police came to take me away for fingerprints and mug shots, I realised too late that I had become a single mother.

Darryl Fowler and the Mistaken Identity Case

The train pulled to a halt at a stop sign just outside Birmingham New Street station. This seemed like a good moment for me to check my suitcase. Birmingham was my stop and on the journey from Cardiff I had spread things from my backpack over the table on the train – my netbook, a magazine, lunch, my mp3 player – and now I needed to gather them up and rescue my suitcase from the luggage rack before the train sped on towards Manchester.

I always carry the essentials in my backpack and I did have some difficulty jamming the netbook in between my washbag and a small towel, but the pack went on my back and I was striding down the carriage to the luggage rack as the train lurched forwards.

At the luggage rack though, my suitcase was not there. There was a rucksack, a brown Gladstone bag and a small, curvier suitcase with a blue handle but there was no sign of my suitcase, which was square, black and had a red handle. Sometimes I do look in the wrong luggage rack, so I quickly turned around and fought against the tide of people coming the other way towards the exit. However, at the other end of the carriage there was no suitcase of mine either. I swore under my breath and pushed my way back to the original luggage rack. This was definitely where I had left my suitcase. I looked around wildly. Where the hell had it gone?

A young woman sitting across the aisle asked me what was wrong, spotting the look of panic on my face.

I said that my suitcase had disappeared. She asked what it looked like and I described it as black, square and with a red handle. She helped look. I am not sure why she was helping me, other than that I must have exuded an air of desperation and she seemed like one of those friendly student types always willing to help out (looking back now, why she had not got off at University station just before New Street I am not sure).

We searched one luggage rack after another but there was no sign.

"I was getting off at New Street," I said.

"Will you stay on the train to find it or get off before the train leaves?" she asked, sounding genuinely concerned.

"I don't know," I said.

The train was standing at the platform now waiting for new passengers and I had no idea what to do. My weekend in Birmingham was possible without my suitcase, but what if it was on the train somewhere still?

"Excuse me," said a voice from a group of older ladies sitting at the far end of the carriage.

I walked over and saw that the one who was speaking was a short woman with grey hair sticking out from under a green woollen hat. I said hello, sharply and without patience.

"I think that the man who was here took it," she said, indicating a seat opposite the group of the four women, "he was talking about getting off at University."

Her friends nodded their agreement. One of them with dyed dark hair and a beige winter coat added some more detail.

"Yes, he had a suitcase with a red handle by his side. He was talking about sneaking away to meet his girlfriend somewhere," she said.

Again, the group of four agreed. He had definitely been visiting his girlfriend and he had had a suitcase with a red handle that he had pulled off the luggage rack just before the train reached University station.

"It was a conference in Manchester he should have been at," said the first woman again, "I remember. Very polite young man."

"Thank you," I said, "that's a great help."

"I hope you find your case – perhaps his is still on the rack."

It was a puzzle but luckily I was a man who liked puzzles. What did we have so far? A man had taken my suitcase at University and was now heading for a weekend with his girlfriend. I suspected that he was aged around forty in that the older women had called him 'young man'. I still enjoyed being called 'young man' at forty and it would be nice to think that they were complimenting me by extension.

"It must be his case," said the student, who was now standing by the luggage rack again. People do like a mystery, I thought.

"Okay Watson," I replied, "can you ask the people in this carriage if theirs is the black suitcase with the blue handle and we will go from there?"

She smiled and seemed happy with her promotion to my assistant. She bounced off down the carriage asking the Friday evening travellers about their luggage. It took the confidence of youth to do that or perhaps it took the confidence of a cute young woman who does not yet realise how many people only talk to her because she is a cute young woman. She returned and told me that no-one claimed ownership of it.

The train had left New Street by this point, so I decided that it was time to find out a bit more about who had taken my identity. I pulled the case down from the luggage rack and took it to a table, my assistant following happily behind me. I heard one of the older women mutter, "he's going to open it!"

The first thing that I did was check the tag on the outside of the suitcase. All it said was 'John Williams' which did, at least, give me a name. I slipped a hand into the outside zip pocket and pulled out some papers. This was promising. They were a travel itinerary for going from Cardiff to Manchester, a print out of a hotel reservation for the Manchester Midland Hotel and paper copies of some e-mails about a conference. I knew how that worked. I always put my travel documents in the outside of my suitcase too, making the interesting thought that somewhere in Birmingham, John Williams was doing just the same thing with my suitcase.

I looked at my assistant and she shook her head.

"You can't open it," she said.

"How else am I going to find him? This is obviously the official paperwork of what he was supposed to be doing this weekend, but how can I find him if he hasn't got a note of where he has actually gone?" I asked.

She shook her head. She had that half-curly, half-wavy hair that would have taken an age to control if she had wanted it straight, but which she left as a kind of stylish mess and shaking her head left it over her face. She pushed it away with a hand and stared at me as if I was clueless.

"You've got his hotel booking. Go to the hotel and he is bound to call you when he discovers that he has the wrong case," she said.

I had to admit that that sounded convincing to me. I had one last worry about committing an act of theft, however.

"Is there anyone on this train called 'John Williams'?" I announced loudly.

There was no answer until one of the older women said, "John Williams? Isn't he a composer? Was that the man we were talking to?"

"Thank you," I said to my student assistant, "it looks like I am going to Manchester."

* * * * *

It is hard to explain what sitting in Manchester Piccadilly station is like if you are from Wales. The three million people who call Wales home are spread out across a large area and even our capital city is small compared to the big cities of England. I had been to Manchester before, but even now I felt slightly overwhelmed by the sheer volume of people. Yes, Cardiff has a hinterland of Valleys who send their youngest and drunkest to work in the city during the week and to drink in the city at the weekend, but it is still not that simple volume of human beings in one place that you find in England.

Manchester is simply more diverse than Cardiff too. I did not think twice about the receptionist at the Midland Hotel being a man with accented English and a Latvian flag pin badge on his lapel, nor did I question that the security guard was black. It is not that Cardiff does not have a mix of people, it is just that you are more aware of it in English cities.

Of course, it was the diversity that had brought me to Manchester for big weekends too. I would not go as far as my friend who unkindly said that a night out in Cardiff was about tripping over drunken women from the Valleys falling out of taxis, but the scene in Manchester was different. However, I was not here for a holiday, I was here by mistake.

"John Williams," I had said to the receptionist in the hotel and Sandis (his name badge said) scanned through the bookings and replied that they had the room for me that I had booked. I wanted to say that I had not booked it, but I felt that I could do without having to explain too much.

"One thing Sandis," I said, hoping that using his first name would make me seem less suspicious, "there has been a bit of a mix up so if another John Williams comes in here, especially looking for his suitcase, can you let me know?"

The mark of a good hotel is that when you ask them the most ridiculous request, they simply nod and say 'very good, Sir'. Last time I was staying in Manchester I dropped a drinking glass in the bathroom and when I returned from breakfast, the glass had simply been cleared away and it was never mentioned. A good hotel understands service or possibly I was unused to staying in good hotels and remained easily impressed.

I found my room and it seemed likable enough. The first thing I did there was make a mug of tea. I love the way that all British hotels have a kettle and tea-making facilities. You can find them in a B&B in Margate, you can find them in the poshest hotel in London, British people always have to have access to tea. I even knew a man who was sent to a mental hospital many years ago and reportedly when asked about what it was like complained that there were no tea and coffee making facilities.

The big question was what to do with the suitcase. Of course, the first hour was easy, I simply sat next to it and watched television. Yet the more I thought about it, the more I asked myself why John Williams would come to Manchester to look for it. He was now in a hotel somewhere in Birmingham with his girlfriend and probably having a laugh at my novelty underwear. Why would he tell her that he had to waste half a day or more of their time together to find me? In fact, would he have simply thought that the train would have reached Manchester and the suitcase would be handed in as lost property? I had to open it.

Inside the internal zip pocket was an alarm clock, about three of four chargers tangled up together, a book and some pyjamas. These were obviously the night things to put out in the hotel room. In the main case were a pair of jeans, a jumper, a change of shoes and some smart clothes at the bottom. I wanted to hang them up to stop them becoming too creased and then I wondered why on earth I was taking care of another man's clothes! The gold in that mine though was an A4 notepad and the papers clipped to it inviting John Williams of Acorn Cosmetics to the 'Iberia '18 Hair & Beauty Conference' at the King's House Conference Centre, Manchester. This was where John Williams would be or at least would have been had he not been using it as an excuse to see his girlfriend.

It was only then that I did something that I should probably have done before. I took out my phone and searched online for 'John Williams'. Perhaps subconsciously I knew what the result was going to be – almost every hit was the American composer of the 'Star Wars' music. Can you imagine how many Star Wars websites there are where he is mentioned? That was an obvious dead end – why had the suitcase snatcher not been called Zebedee Arnold for heaven's sake? That would have been too easy. I searched for Zebedee Arnold. Apparently he married one of the passengers on 'The Lion' which sailed from England to Boston in 1632. The internet has so many ways to waste your time.

Oddly enough, I could not find 'Acorn Cosmetics' either. That was stranger. There were a lot of cosmetics made out of acorns, but no company. Perhaps they only sold to trade, perhaps they were too small, but it was becoming increasingly clear that my only possible link was the conference. John Williams was not going to turn up at my hotel that night. I even checked with Sandis before he went off shift but no-one had been in contact. I went out for a beer.

Sitting at a bar on Canal Street, I pondered my options. I could go home to Cardiff, admit defeat and phone the train company to ask about lost property. I could go to Birmingham and wander around looking for a man whose description I barely knew. I could stay in Manchester and give myself the weekend to work it out. It had to be the last option. I like puzzles and I was sure that there was something that I was missing. There had to be.

* * * * *

I slept naked, not wanting to wear another man's pyjamas. However, on the Saturday morning I felt that I had no choice but to wear the smart clothes that I had hung up the night before. I was going to the conference. It seemed an odd thing to do but it also seemed like the only way to find out a bit more about the mysterious Mr Williams. I was also enjoying the strange case a little too much. If I met him then I would excuse wearing his clothes as the only way to meet him, if I found a link for him then I could pack away his clothes before I gave him back his suitcase.

"Mr Williams," said the woman at the entrance to the hotel restaurant that morning and I turned around to look for him before I realised that she was matching my room number to her list of people who I had booked breakfast, "full breakfast, table four."

"Vegetarian breakfast," I corrected her.

"Oh, I am sorry, Sir" she said, "we did not have that correctly listed. Please do inform your waiter of your dietary requirements."

Nothing is ever too much trouble in these hotels, no wonder John Williams is booked into them!

To be honest, breakfast gave me a chance to work out a bit more about the man I was now imitating. He was about my size and fit in terms of the clothes, thank goodness, and he was a carnivore. This did not really help but it gave me some idea that I was learning more about him. I walked to the conference centre unsure of my strategy other than turning up late into the early morning networking to give him a chance to get there first. Would he be wearing my blue t-shirt with 'Do me a kindness' written across the front?

However, when I reached the conference centre and found the floor for the hair and beauty conference, I spotted a badge with his name on it lying on the table at the entrance.

"Which badge are you looking at?" asked the young woman behind the table, clearing noticing that my gaze had been caught by one of them.

"John Williams," I said, pointing at the badge, "Acorn Cosmetics."

The young woman had her own badge saying 'Rebecca, Iberia '18' and a list of all the people who should be in the event. She ticked me off the list and passed me the badge. I had to head off any future misunderstandings.

"There has been a bit of a mix-up this weekend between me and another John Williams," I tried to explain as if it were the most normal thing in the world, "if someone comes along saying that they are also John Williams, can you let me know?"

Rebecca's job was clearly to sit behind the desk and tick people off the list, she was not prepared for strange men telling her that they had a double or a namesake or whatever I was claiming. She had a pretty smile and she fought hard to maintain it as she tried to make sense of me.

"Your company sent two representatives with the same name?" she asked.

"Not exactly, but there has been a bit of a mix-up."

"We only have one John Williams booked," she said, scanning her list of Johns or possibly Williamses, I was unsure which order her list was in.

A group of middle-aged women had appeared behind me and although they had exchanged greetings of 'I haven't seen you since Reykjavik!' or similar conference-goer talk, they were now becoming a little bit restless about being kept from the networking. Rebecca could sense this and was clearly keen to move me into the networking room as politely and efficiently as possible. I saw a chance.

"Look, perhaps if I could talk to the organiser, I could explain to her?" I tried.

"Sam? Yes, that would be best. Over there," she said, pointing to a harassed-looking young man with a mop of curly hair, standing in the middle of a predominantly female crowd of delegates.

"Thank you," I said and as I moved off, I could hear the women behind me greet Rebecca as if they were old friends.

Sam was a nervous young man with a kind of intensity of purpose which I might have expected from a political activist, not a conference organiser. When I said hello and asked if I could have a word with me, he responded with, "is it about the vegan food?"

"No, I have no problem with the food," I replied.

"Good. Thank goodness. It was a problem in the catering. We always have the dietary requirements spot on, but someone mixed up the orders and ..."

He had a walkie talkie in his hand and I thought to myself that he might not have had the build of a security guard, but he had the air of someone who was working hard to keep everything together and that he knew people who could have you ejected from the building if you caused trouble.

"I wanted to check if you had my company's details correctly on your files," I tried, my aim being to find the details and phone Acorn Cosmetics for a contact number for John Williams.

"Data protection? Oh, we take it very seriously," he replied.

"Err ... this is going to sound a bit rude, but could I check them now – you know, before the day starts? We moved address recently and I really want to make sure it is correct. Would you do me a kindness and check for me?"

Sam looked startled and unsure. I smiled. I am told that I have a friendly face and a kind smile. I think that this is why young women on trains help me look for my missing suitcase and I was hoping that it would help a thirty something man with a walkie talkie help me find out the contact details for the company who employed me. Really I hoped that it would make him not think through what I was asking him.

"Now?" he asked.

"It is important to us," I replied.

Perhaps they have a saying at conferences along the lines of 'the delegate is always right' but I saw him hesitate, think about it and then finally decide that the best way to keep me away from him was to take out a battered-looking phone and dial a number into it.

"Sally?" he said into the phone, "Can you do me a favour? I'm going to hand you over to the guy from – hold on – Acorn Cosmetics, he needs to check the details on file. Could you sort it?"

Sally obviously agreed because after a few moments he passed me his phone. He then resumed looking around the room and giving off an air of agitation about whether people were going to stick to the timings for the day. I explained to Sally what I needed and she read out the following –

"It's your first booking with us, so all we have for you is Acorn Cosmetics, 02920 792638 and John Williams. If you were moving then your secretary probably said that you could fill in the new details for us today."

"Thank you Sally, you have been most helpful."

As I thanked Sally and then thanked Sam my head was desperately repeating 792638 in the hope that I would remember it long enough to write it down. I did not want to do it in front of Sam in case he wondered why I had to write down a phone number that I should know. As it was, once I handed the phone back, Sam did not have another minute for me as he was asking Sally about the catering arrangements and I could give a hesitant wave as a goodbye.

You can imagine that as soon as I found a free space, I tapped 02920 792638 into my phone. It rang for what seemed like an age but then there was a click and a cheery, female voice greeted me with "Hello Acorn Cosmetics, *Shwmae Acorn Cosmetics*."

"Hello, my name's Darryl Fowler and I'm trying ..."

"Our business hours are nine to five, Monday to Friday. If you would like to leave a message for us outside these times, along with your name and contact details, we will get back to you as soon as we can. To hear this information in Welsh, please press two."

She sounded somehow familiar, but maybe I was just missing hearing Welsh voices already. At least I knew that Acorn existed, though the lack of website and now being closed at weekends led me to believe that they were a small company. That should play into my favour in terms of tracking down John Williams, but my aim had been to do it this weekend. I thought that I might as well leave them a message.

"Hello, my name Darryl Fowler and I am trying to contact one of your employees, John Williams. I may have accidentally picked up his suitcase and he may have mine. Could you ask him to call me urgently on 07789 542324? Thank you."

Back to square one, I thought and without really knowing what to do next, I went into the opening presentation.

After ten minutes, I could tell you everything there was to know about the challenges of expanding markets in cosmetics, especially in Asia. I did introduce myself – or rather introduce John Williams - to some of the other delegates, but no-one seemed to know him and I had the impression that Acorn Cosmetics were not seen as a big player in the market. Someone from Elemis or one of those other big cosmetics companies complained to me about having to translate a marketing banner they put up in a school in Cardiff into Welsh. One of the other men there (and we were noticeable by our scarcity) told me that there was 'room for men like us' in hair and beauty, which threw me a little. I decided that at the lunch break, I would leave discreetly. This was not helping me further and the clock was ticking.

Back at the hotel, I checked with Sandis that there were no messages for John Williams and returned to my room. I opened up the suitcase again and this time tipped out all of its contents across the bed. There had to be a clue that I was missing. Perhaps the cosmetics angle was a red herring? What does someone's suitcase say about them?

I checked the pockets of the clothes, but they were all empty. The information for the conference and the train tickets also told me very little. All I had left to check was the pile of chargers and the book. I am not a reader. I mean, show me a book and I will ask you when the film is coming out. I know that I should read, but it always seems so slow compared to catching up with the latest box set on Netflix. My partner is a reader and always tells me that I should look at books more. In fact, before I had left on this trip, my partner had said that I should pay more attention to books, but I have never been persuaded that it would benefit my life.

What was this book that John Williams had brought with him? "A Very British Coup" by Chris Mullin. I had never heard of it. It had a 'thriller' sticker on it and it came from the library in Cardiff, but beyond that I could not think that it was much help. However, it must have been a little desperation setting in because I started to run my hands along the outside of the pages. The book fell open at a white piece of paper tucked in to the middle of the book.

I picked out the paper, letting the book fall out of my hands and close. One side of the paper was covered in doodles and I thought that I had an idea what this was. I know that not everyone has a landline these days and that many of them who do have a landline have a mobile handset, but some people like me have a fixed phone in the corner of the front room for official calls. Looking at the paper, I thought that maybe this was true of John Williams too.

If you have a mobile phone, what do you do if you are in your house and someone gives you some important information? You say 'oh hold on, let me get a pen' and rush around the house looking for a pen and a piece of paper. What do you do if you have a landline? You are fixed to one spot, so you have a pad of paper sitting by the phone so you can write down important messages. What do you then do if you are sitting by the phone? You doodle. John Williams had doodled all over this piece of paper and, perhaps thinking that he would no longer need it, he had then used it as a bookmark.

The doodles were the usual checkerboard pattern, balls of lightening, a couple of sets of initials and then something that really caught my attention – 'Springfield

Road, Birmingham (get off at University)' written at the bottom. Had he been on the phone to his girlfriend and needed to note where he was going and which station to leave the train from?

Honestly, it was a moment where the mystery suddenly came alive again. I switched on my phone and opened an app that searched company addresses. Sure enough, there was a Springfield Road and no fewer than thirty-seven hotels or B&Bs listed along its route. The clock showed that we were getting on for three o'clock, it was going to be an afternoon of talking to hotel owners!

You can imagine how the first call went –

"Hello, is that Sedgwick Hotel?"

"Yes, this is Mrs Sedgwick speaking."

"Hi, I'd like to know if you have a John Williams staying with you this weekend."

"I'm sorry Sir, we cannot give out guest information."

Thwarted by data protection! I had to change my tack and hope that the first one was not the one where John Williams was staying. I decided that he might be trying to impress his girlfriend, so I started with the most expensive hotels and this time I rang up and asked to be put through to John Williams, claiming to be the Managing Director of Acorn Cosmetics. The first five attempts all had a confused equivalent of Sandis saying that there was no John Williams staying with them, was I sure about the name? Then I would apologise profusely and claim that I had meant to call a different hotel.

I will admit that the excitement wore off a bit after four o'clock, but then I struck gold. The Bournville View Hotel said that they would try to connect me to Mr Williams's room. The phone rang ... and no-one picked up. I pondered what to do next. I could not let this trail go cold, so I asked the receptionist (Maria) if she would take a message for him explaining that I had picked up his suitcase and that he had mine and that we needed to meet to exchange them. I gave her my contact details in the Midland Hotel and asked for Mr Williams to call me urgently.

It was only when I put the phone down that I realised that he might not be the right Mr Williams! What could I do then? I walked down to reception and let Sandis know that I might be receiving a call. Then I decided to walk around to Manchester Cathedral, to take a ride on the trams, visit the Lowry Centre ... basically to enjoy Manchester thinking that maybe I had come a big step closer to solving the mystery of the mistaken suitcase.

To cut this story short, I had a message when I returned to the hotel to tell me that Mr Williams had called and he would be travelling to the hotel on Sunday morning. I was relieved, though I had expected to have to travel to Birmingham. I took my time that night to enjoy a night out in Manchester before returning to my room and re-packing his case as nearly as I could do.

* * * * *

I was standing in the reception talking to Sandis after a hearty vegetarian breakfast when I heard him come through the door.

"Mr Williams!" he announced, dragging a suitcase with a red handle.

He looked handsome. Dark-haired, well-built and with a big smile beaming at me. He walked forwards and kissed me fully on the lips.

"Thank goodness you got here!" I said, putting an arm around him and drawing him to my side.

I looked over at Sandis and he was staring at us. No wonder really, we needed to explain what was going on.

"He's not really John Williams," I said, causing Sandis's brow to furrow even deeper, "he's my partner Tim."

"Hi!" said Tim, "This one loves puzzles and I like setting them so, each year I devise one for him."

"Yes," I continued without needing there to be a break between our sentences, "he just tells me where to go and then swaps my suitcase at some point as a challenge to find him. And can I say - bloody hell, in a book!"

"What did I say to you before you left?" Tim asked, giving me a hug, "You will get more from books than you imagine. You're never listening!"

"But you are expecting it when it happens?" asked Sandis, disturbing our hugging.

"That was a problem the first couple of times," I admitted, "people only really help if I can panic convincingly."

"Ah, my great actor," said Tim and planted a kiss on my forehead.

"The message on the phone - that was your sister, right?" I asked.

"Yes," he said, still not letting go of my arm, "she had a free hotel in Birmingham out of it, so she won't complain. Thought you might recognise her voice. Did you go to the conference?"

I slapped him on the arm playfully, "Yes and what a red herring. Should have made up a website for them though."

"Next time, next time ..." muttered Tim, already thinking of the next puzzle.

"Ahem," said Sandis with a cough, disturbing our jolly reunion, "will you be checking out?"

"Ah what the hell," I said, "let's stay here a little longer, I've got used to it!"

Tim laughed and kissed me again.

"Happy birthday," he said.

AFTERWORD

Thanks for reading this book, I hope that you enjoyed it.

If you have nice things to say then please send an e-mail to dewiheald@gmail.com

You can also follow me on Twitter @DewiHeald1

And on Instagram – thebooksandmusicofdewiheald

If you did not enjoy this collection of random thoughts and writings, then you should contact our complaints service by writing to -

Rt Hon Theresa May MP

10, Downing Street

London

SW1A 0AA

You can also buy other books from my bookshop -

http://dewiheald.wixsite.com/rainbows/books

This book has been made possible by the support and efforts of a large number of people, to whom I remain and will always be, grateful.

please
colour
in this
page

www.ingramcontent.com/pod-product-compliance
Lightning Source LLC
Chambersburg PA
CBHW061319040426
42444CB00011B/2710